SNAPSHOTS
from the Book of
REVELATION

THEODORE C. DANSON SMITH

Ambassador International
Greenville, South Carolina • Belfast, Northern Ireland
www.ambassador-international.com
Celebrating Forty Years of Getting the Word Around

Snapshots from the Book of Revelation

©2019 by Theodore C. Danson Smith
All rights reserved

ISBN: 978-1-62020-952-3
eISBN: 978-1-62020-964-6

Cover Design and Page Layout by Hannah Nichols
eBook Conversion by Anna Riebe Raats

Scripture quotations taken from The King James Version. The Authorized Version. Public Domain.

AMBASSADOR INTERNATIONAL
Emerald House
411 University Ridge, Suite B14
Greenville, SC 29601, USA
www.ambassador-international.com

AMBASSADOR BOOKS
The Mount
2 Woodstock Link
Belfast, BT6 8DD, Northern Ireland, UK
www.ambassadormedia.co.uk

The colophon is a trademark of Ambassador, a Christian publishing company.

DEDICATION

I dedicate this book to the two men who influenced my life tremendously.

The first is my dear father – J Danson Smith – whose poems are known around the world. He taught me the Word of God from babyhood, and at an early age he encouraged me to study Bible prophecy.

The other is Dr David J. Laurie. His outstanding preaching and his tremendous burden for lost souls shaped my life and inspired my preaching.

Both of them are in the Glory Land, and I look forward to seeing them in the Rapture and thanking them.

Maranatha!

—Theodore C. Danson Smith

CONTENTS

DEDICATION 3

PREFACE 7

CHAPTER ONE
ALPHA AND OMEGA 9

CHAPTER TWO
THE HISTORY OF THE CHURCH 17

CHAPTER THREE
COME UP HITHER 27

CHAPTER FOUR
THE BOOK OF REDEMPTION 35

CHAPTER FIVE
THE FOUR HORSEMEN 43

CHAPTER SIX
THE GREAT TRIBULATION 51

CHAPTER SEVEN
THE 144,000 61

CHAPTER EIGHT
SILENCE IN HEAVEN 69

CHAPTER NINE
GOD'S TWO WITNESSES 77

CHAPTER TEN
ISRAEL AND THE DRAGON 85

CHAPTER ELEVEN
THE TWO BEASTS 93

CHAPTER TWELVE
JUDGMENT PREDICTED 101

CHAPTER THIRTEEN
THE SEVEN VIAL JUDGMENTS 109

CHAPTER FOURTEEN
THE DOOM OF THE VATICAN 117

CHAPTER FIFTEEN
POLITICAL BABYLON 125

CHAPTER SIXTEEN
THE WEDDING OF THE AGES 135

CHAPTER SEVENTEEN
ARMAGEDDON 143

CHAPTER EIGHTEEN
THE GREAT WHITE THRONE 151

CHAPTER NINETEEN
THE NEW HEAVEN AND THE NEW EARTH 159

CHAPTER TWENTY
A TREMENDOUS VERSE 167

CHAPTER TWENTY-ONE
THE NEW JERUSALEM 175

CHAPTER TWENTY-TWO
THE BEGINNING AND THE END 183

ABOUT THE AUTHOR 191

PREFACE

The Book of Revelation is a closed book to many people. In it the apostle John has given a preview of the end times in which we are now living. It is important to understand that the Lord has two distinctly separate peoples – His *earthly* people, Israel, and His *heavenly* people, the Church.

In Revelation the Church is seen in chapters 1,2, 3 and chapter 4 verse 1. It reappears again in chapters 19 to 22. The other chapters deal with Israel and the nations.

This book is not a commentary but it gives various snapshots to encourage readers to understand and enjoy this thrilling book. The contents were preached in meetings all over the United Kingdom.

The reader needs to be certain that his or her salvation has been obtained through faith in the atoning blood of the Lord Jesus Christ. The Bible says 'The blood of Jesus Christ His Son cleanseth us from all sin' (1 John 1:7).

CHAPTER ONE

ALPHA AND OMEGA

Reading: Revelation chapter 1

Text: Revelation 1:8 – 'I am Alpha and Omega, the beginning and the ending.'

INTRODUCTION

The Book of the Revelation is a closed book to many people because they simply do not understand it. However it is one of the greatest books in the Bible. The key to understanding it is found in v. 19 of chapter 1: 'Write the things which thou hast seen, and the things which are, and the things which shall be hereafter.' In other words, we have here the PAST, the PRESENT and the FUTURE. This chapter deals mainly with the Lord Jesus Christ – hence our text – 'I am Alpha and Omega, the beginning and the ending.' Christ is the central theme of the Bible and this book and chapter 1 in particular is all about Him. Do you, my friend, know Him? Is He your Saviour?

This chapter commences with the apostle John telling how he was in the Spirit on the Lord's Day. This would be better rendered 'The Day of the Lord.' In other words, he was given a peep into the future to see what will happen in the 'Day of the Lord' which is yet future. To begin with though, He sees the Lord Jesus Christ – the 'Alpha and the Omega' – the One Who is first and last. This vision of the Saviour is known as 'the things which thou hast seen' – namely the PAST. Then, he is given a picture of the PRESENT – the Church Age – with a seven-fold description of it, and finally he sees the FUTURE

– 'the things which shall be hereafter.' This last part is known as 'The Day of the Lord.'

In this message, we shall look at chapter 1 only. 'I am the Alpha and Omega, the beginning and the ending.' Notice first of all:-

CHRIST'S PERSON

The apostle John sees the Lord Jesus Christ in all His glory. On earth He was 'The Son of Man' which speaks somewhat of His *humanity*. He was like a *prophet*. When He ascended to heaven He took His humanity with Him and there He intercedes for His people, thus showing His *priesthood*. When Christ returns in power and glory – which is described in chapter 19 – we see Him as *king*. Yes, the Lord Jesus Christ is Prophet, Priest and King!

Here in Revelation chapter 1, the apostle John sees the Lord and hears Him say 'I am the Alpha and Omega, the beginning and the ending.' John sees Him in His glorified state. Verse 5 describes Him as 'the faithful witness' and also as 'the first begotten of the dead.' We know that the Lord Jesus Christ conquered death and rose from the tomb after three days and nights. He is alive for evermore. He is a living Saviour and saves people today. More than that, He is 'prince of the kings of the earth.' The day is coming when His kingdom will stretch from shore to shore, and He will reign supreme over the whole earth for a thousand years. Daniel sees the Lord Jesus Christ as 'King of heaven' (Daniel 4:37). Matthew proclaims Him as 'King of the Jews' (Matthew 2:2). John speaks of Him in his Gospel as 'King of Israel (John 1:49). Paul refers to Him in 1 Timothy 1:17 as 'King of the ages.' Psalm 24:7 calls Him 'The King of Glory.'

Christ's Person is wonderful. John is overwhelmed. And he bursts into a peon of praise: 'Unto Him that loved us, and washed us from our sins in His own blood.' Can I ask, friend, are *you* washed in that precious blood? His blood was shed for us poor, lost sinners. Oh, what love He showed in coming from heaven to save us!

> The love of God is greater far
> Than tongue or pen can ever tell;
> It goes beyond the highest star
> And reaches to the lowest hell.

'I am the Alpha and Omega, the beginning and the ending.' Let us look, secondly at:-

CHRIST'S POSITION

John sees the Lord 'in the midst of the seven candlesticks.' What does this mean? The word 'candlesticks' is shown as 'lamp stands' in the margin, and this really is showing the Lord in relation to the seven churches which will be referred to in chapters 2 and 3. Christ is central in the message of the church – not religion, nor local people or things. The Saviour *must* be central. That is Christ's position.

Light is always needed, and in the Gospels we find that the Lord Jesus is 'the Light of the world' (John 8:12). True Christians should be reflectors of that Light, but we often fail. As the hymn says:-

> The whole world was lost in the darkness of sin,
> The Light of the world is Jesus!
> Like sunshine at noonday His glory shone in,
> The Light of the world is Jesus.

This world of ours is in darkness – terrible darkness. Things are getting darker all the time. Sin is always on the increase, but true Christians have the answer. The Lord Jesus is the Light. He brings the lost ones out of darkness. He brightens lives. He brings the sunshine! Drunks, drug addicts, criminals and lots of very ordinary folk find their darkness transformed when they repent and ask the Lord to save them. The Lord Jesus and He alone is 'the Alpha and Omega, the beginning and the ending.' Do you know Him, friend? Have you been transformed? The message of Revelation chapter 1 is: Look to the Saviour. He is and should always be *central*. That is His rightful position.

Yes, and He ought to be the centre of all our living. 'I am Alpha and Omega, the beginning and the ending.' These two words are the first and last letters of the Greek alphabet and they remind us that the Lord Jesus Christ is the eternal 'I am' – the One Who has always existed. He is the great Creator. As John says in his Gospel: 'All things were made by Him' (John 1: 3). He is also the great controller, as Hebrews 1:3 indicates. Revelation 1:8 tells us that the Lord Jesus is the One 'which is, and which was, and which is to come.'

We have looked briefly at Christ's Person and at Christ's Position. Let us look next at:-

CHRIST'S POWER

'I am Alpha and Omega, the beginning and the ending.' Our text makes it clear that the Lord Jesus Christ truly is first and last. He was there in the beginning. Jesus said in Matthew 28:18 'All power is given unto me.' That power covers heaven and earth, and He then commanded His followers to go into all the world and preach the gospel to everyone. Are we who love the Lord doing that? Do we witness for Him at home, work and wherever we go? His power is available to us today through the indwelling Holy Spirit, but, sadly, most Christians depend on themselves and not on Him. Remember, Christian friends, that power is available to you and to me today.

As we look at John's description of the Lord in this chapter, we see several things of importance. The Lord's head was one of great dignity. His voice was one of great authority. His eyes were as a flame of fire – most powerful and penetrating. From His mouth came a sharp two-edged sword. This sword has a double purpose. It will be used for the destruction of the Lord's enemies, and it will be used also for the protection of His Own dear people. In His hand He held the seven stars. These stars are the ministers, or leaders in the churches. Such men have tremendous responsibility. As faithful servants of the Lord they receive His power and His message to pass on to others, but if they are unfaithful, they will suffer His displeasure.

Our text states 'I am Alpha and Omega, the beginning and the ending.' Christ's power requires that He must be first and last in every true Christian's life. Does He have that position in your life, in mine?

John goes on to describe His appearance. He says 'His countenance was as the sun.' John had already seen that on the Mount of Transfiguration along with Peter and James. Paul saw that brightness on the day when the Lord saved him. He was dazzled. No one may dare stare at the sun in the sky, or they will go blind, but the brightness of the Lord in glory is something yet to be seen. As the old hymn says: 'The Lamb is all the glory in Emmanuel's land.' The Lord Jesus Christ is the most powerful Light in the whole universe.

The prophet Malachi describes the return of the Lord Jesus showing Him as 'the Sun of Righteousness' (Malachi 4:2). He will then be coming in all His glory as Judge of all the earth, and as King of kings and Lord of lords. Christ's power is unmatched. No enemy of His will ever prosper. He is the all-victorious One. He revealed His power to John, for he fell at the Lord's feet, and He told him to arise and write and let the world eventually know what was and is and is to come. 'I am Alpha and Omega, the beginning and the ending.'

Let us have one other glimpse at the Lord Jesus in this chapter. We have seen His Person, His Position and something of His Power. Let us consider finally:-

CHRIST'S PRE-EMINENCE

'I am Alpha and Omega, the beginning and the ending.' Yes, friend, He must be pre-eminent. He is not showing self-praise. No, He is just simply stating facts. In verses 17 and 18 He says to John: 'I am the first and the last: I am He that liveth and was dead; and, behold, I am alive for evermore, Amen; and have the keys of hell and of death.'

The Saviour went to Calvary – to the Cross – because of His love for us. He paid the penalty for our sins. He shed His precious, sinless blood to make atonement for each one of us. He gave up His life, but thank God He arose from the dead – victorious over sin and the grave, and He is 'alive for evermore.' Our relationship to the Lord Jesus decides if we shall eventually go to heaven or to hell. Some people think that a God of love will never send people there, but they are wrong. God sent His only begotten Son into the world to save us from going to hell. His arms were stretched out on the Cross because of His love for sinners. Long ago in the desert in Sinai the people were dying because of snake bites, and God told Moses to make and erect a brass snake in the camp, and all those who were bitten by snakes – if they looked to that brass snake – were healed. Today, all who look in true repentance and faith to the Saviour will be delivered from their sin and saved eternally. Have YOU done this, friend? If not, then 'Now is the accepted time. Behold, now is the day of salvation' (2 Corinthians 6:2). Look to the Lord Jesus NOW and be saved. Our relationship to Him determines our eternal destiny. We shall either go to heaven because He has saved us, or we shall be lost eternally because we go our own way.

> I've a message from the Lord, Hallelujah!
> The message unto you I'll give;
> 'Tis recorded in His Word, Hallelujah!
> It is only that you 'look and live.'
> Look and live, my brother, live!
> Look to Jesus now and live.

Will you do that, friend? This is the look that saves. Hell is the place of never-ending torment and millions are going there. In fact, the majority are going there. You can be saved right now, if you repent and ask the Lord to save you. The Bible says 'Believe on the Lord Jesus Christ and thou shalt be saved' (Acts 16:31). The Bible also says 'Neither is there salvation in any other, for there is none other name under heaven given among men whereby we must be saved' (Acts 4:12). He alone can save.

Christ's pre-eminence. Yes, friend, He is 'the Alpha and Omega, the beginning and the ending.' Some people resent the preaching of the Cross. Many years ago Dr RA Torrey was holding meetings in the Royal Albert Hall and a man cut out all the hymns on the blood from Torrey's hymnbook and sent it to him telling him to leave the blood alone. Torrey's answer was simply that all through the Old and New Testaments the blood is there as the only remedy for sin. The Bible says 'Without shedding of blood there is no remission' (Hebrews 9:22) – no forgiveness. The words of the hymn are so true:-

What can wash away my stain?
Nothing but the blood of Jesus!
What can make me whole again?
Nothing but the blood of Jesus!

Those who ignore the message of salvation and go their own way will meet the Lord Jesus Christ at the Judgment of the Great White Throne, and there they will hear His words 'Depart from Me, I never knew you.' Religion, good works, baptism and so on can *never* save. Only when we come in simple faith and repentance to the Lord will we be heard. The great apostle Paul wrote in his later years from his prison in Rome 'For me to live is Christ' (Philippians 1:21). Christian friend, is the Lord Jesus pre-eminent in your life like that? If not, then now is the moment to hand your all to Him and live henceforth for Him and for Him alone.

CONCLUSION

Let us look once more at our text: 'I am Alpha and Omega, the beginning and the ending.' The dear Lord Jesus is the beginning of *life* for all who repent and believe. He is also the ending for all who already are saved and trusting in Him, for we shall one day go to be with Him for evermore. Paul explains this in Philippians 1. He is coming again any time.

The message of Revelation chapter 1 is this: *Christ is central and supreme.* We either know Him as our personal Saviour, or we shall meet Him as our Judge. Which is it with YOU? Jesus said 'Him that cometh to Me I will in no wise cast out' (John 6:37). Will you come now?

Jesus for your choice is waiting;
Tarry not: at once decide;
While the Spirit now is striving;
Yield, and seek the Saviour's side.

CHAPTER TWO

THE HISTORY OF THE CHURCH

Reading: Revelation 2:1-7 and Revelation 3: 7-22

Text: Revelation 3:20 – 'Behold, I stand at the door, and knock; if any man hear My voice, and open the door, I will come in to him, and will sup with him and he with Me.'

INTRODUCTION

Revelation chapters 2 and 3 portray the history of the church from the apostolic times until the present day. In chapter 1:9 John was told 'Write the things which thou hast seen and the things which are, and the things which shall be hereafter.' What had he seen? In chapter 1 he describes that. It was the Lord Jesus Christ in all His glory. 'The things which are' refers to the Church Age from the time of John until the Rapture of the Church when the Lord Jesus returns to the air and removes His people from a Christ-rejecting world. This period is very simply divided into seven periods. This word 'seven' appears many times in the book of Revelation. The whole Church Age falls into seven periods, and we shall look at these briefly. Each section is different, and while the Lord's message to these seven local churches was applicable to them, it had a *prophetic* message for each period of time that they cover. When the message to the last church – Laodicea – is finished, we have the Rapture of the church in Chapter 4:1,2. Our text, which is often used with a Gospel meaning, is in reality addressed to the Church – 'Behold,

I stand at the door and knock . . . ' Today, in so many places of worship, the Lord Jesus Christ is *outside*. Men and women want to do their own thing, leaving the Lord and His word aside. Jesus is wanting and waiting to be invited in, just as He is waiting to save lost sinners. 'Behold, I stand at the door and knock . . . ' Is He knocking at someone's heart today?

The first church dealt with in Revelation 2 is:-

THE FAULTY CHURCH

Ephesus was a *faulty* church. It was the early apostolic church. It started off well and stood firmly for the truth. Ephesus was the coastal capital of Turkey or Asia Minor. It was a great commercial city and religious centre. The apostle Paul founded this church and spent three years with the people, teaching them and building them up in the faith. It was an active church. It was evangelistic, and it was separated also from the error of the day. Acts 19 reveals how the believers in Ephesus were persecuted and hated, and how trade unions sought to drive them away, but they battled on for the truth. They spotted deceivers in their midst, and we too ought to be aware that the devil sends in his agents into the churches to pose as angels of light, and once they are accepted, they do Satan's work.

How then is this a *faulty church*? Verse 4 has the answer. 'Nevertheless, I have somewhat against thee, because thou hast left thy first love.' This church was sound in doctrine, busy for the Lord and separated also, but they had lost their first love. The Lord Jesus Christ said in Matthew 24:12 'The love of many shall wax cold.' Isn't it true of so many Christians that when they are first saved they are really keen? They rejoice that they have been saved from going to hell. They have been saved eternally and made secure. Through time they grow cold. Are we, perhaps, like that? 'Thou hast left thy first love.' Now is the time to rectify that and ask the Lord to renew our zeal and give us a passion to win the lost. Yes, Ephesus was a faulty church.

Let us look, secondly, at the next church. It is Smyrna:-

THE HISTORY OF THE CHURCH

A FRAGRANT CHURCH

This church period covers roughly AD 100 to 300. For those 200 years the Lord's church suffered severe persecution. Smyrna was another seaport, about 40 miles north of Ephesus. Its main product was myrrh. This was used for making perfume and also for embalming the bodies of the dead. It seems that the Christian witness in Smyrna was the most persecuted of all the churches. However, despite all the persecution, this was a *fragrant church*. The dear people suffered much persecution. They lost many of their possessions, but they were rich in Christ. They kept Him first. As the Bible says in verse 9: 'I know thy works, and tribulation, and poverty, (but thou art rich).' They were rich in following their Saviour and standing fast in all their troubles. These extended from the time of Nero to the death of Domitian and all the Roman emperors in between. The Christian church in that era stood firm. Whatever happened, they would not surrender the truth. And the Lord gave the church at Smyrna this wonderful promise: 'Be thou faithful unto death, and I will give thee a crown of life.' This was the Martyr's Crown. And, we know that thousands of Christians were martyred. Would you, Christian friend, stand firm today, if the European Union demanded that you give up your faith or die? This may happen, if the Lord tarries. The church at Smyrna was a *fragrant church*. The sweetness of their faith impacted on a Christ-rejecting world. Listen to the words of the hymn:-

> Who is on the Lord's side? Who will serve the King?
> Who will be His helpers, other lives to bring?
> Who will leave the world's side? Who will face the foe?
> Who is on the Lord's side? Who for Him will go?
> Fierce may be the conflict, strong may be the foe;
> But the King's own army none can over throw;
> Round His standard ranging, victory is secure
> For His truth unchanging makes the triumph sure.

Friend, when we are saved, we are on the winning side! We may suffer at times, but the sweetness of our faith in the Saviour should be felt by others. 'Behold, I stand at the door and knock.' The Lord is there – always!

The third church is Pergamos. It was:-

A FAITHLESS CHURCH

Pergamos typifies the period of church history from around AD 300 to AD 500. Pergamos was a religious centre. Attalus III was priest king of the Chaldeans, but when the Persians attacked and defeated him he fled to Pergamos, taking with him the religion of Babylon and Baal worship. It is interesting to note that God had two main complaints against this church – 'the doctrine of Balaam' and 'the doctrine of the Nicolaitans.' What exactly were these two doctrines? Balaam was employed by Balak, king of Moab. The story is told in Numbers 22-25. Balak wished Balaam to curse Israel, the people of God, but the Lord would not permit this, so Balaam wickedly suggested to Balak that he invite Israel to some of his religious feasts. These feasts were full of immorality and thousands of God's people sinned, and as a result the Lord killed 42,000 of them.

Pergamos, the *faithless church,* now had entered into a similar situation. This church became much involved in their pagan town. Religion is not the answer to man's need. No. It is the Gospel that Jesus saves! Yes, He saves 'to the uttermost all the come unto God by Him' (Hebrews 7:25).

What is the sin or 'doctrine of the Nicolaitans'? Constantine, the Emperor, decided to join together both church and state, and he created various offices. He had great buildings erected. The leaders in the Church, such as Bishops, Pastors and Elders were given much prominence. He provided these leaders with money and grand garments and in many cases these bishops found themselves sitting on thrones in their large buildings. Popery had commenced. The church was now married to the world. The Lord was outside.

Today, in the ecumenical movement, we have the same thing. This is simply an attempt to unite all churches together and join them in such a way that the state will control them. We know from later chapters in Revelation that this will happen under the Antichrist and False Prophet. Today, popery is using the European Union to destroy true Protestantism and the true gospel. Can I ask, friend, are you saved? Are you trusting the Lord Jesus for salvation? Remember, the church CANNOT save. Only Christ can. The Bible says 'Whosoever shall call on the name of the Lord shall be saved' (Romans 10:13).

Pergamos was a *faithless church*. Let us look next at Thyatira:-

A FOOLISH CHURCH

This church period in history runs from approximately the year 500 to AD 1400. Thyatira was an industrial place. It was famous for its dyeing, pottery, bronze works and so on. It was a busy place and it was to the church there that the Lord sent a message. He knew their love, their patience, their works and their service, but, while these things were good, they were a *foolish church*. They had allowed some woman to lead and teach error and wicked things. She taught them to commit fornication and to eat food offered to idols. God's Word is absolutely clear about such matters. Bible teachers believe that, while this woman was a real, active person in the church at Thyatira, God was also warning the world about the dangers of Roman Catholicism. Rome introduced the worship of Mary and taught that sinners had to go through her to approach the Lord. Poor Mary was just a sinner, like ourselves. She was indeed privileged to bring the Lord Jesus Christ into this world, but In Luke 1:47 she speaks of rejoicing 'in God my Saviour.' Mary needed saving – just as we do individually today. Is there someone reading this perhaps who is not yet saved? Now is the time to repent and ask the Lord Jesus Christ to save you and cleanse you with His precious blood.

> Would you be free from your burden of sin?
> There's power in the blood, power in the blood;

Would you o'er evil a victory win?
There's wonderful power in the blood.

Our text says 'Behold, I stand at the door and knock.' Is the Lord Jesus knocking at *your* heart's door today?

It was in the church period which we can call Thyatira that Roman Catholicism with its worship of Mary, the blasphemous mass and all its many other perversions came into full swing. What a *foolish church*. They had the truth, but allowed a woman – Jezebel – locally, and Romanism, worldwide, to take control.

The fifth church is Sardis:-

A FORMAL CHURCH

The Sardis period of the church runs from 1520 to around AD 1750. It covers the period of the Reformation, when Martin Luther and others rebelled against Roman Catholicism and turned to the Scriptures. This was important, for Romanism did not allow her people to read the Bible. By this means they kept their followers ignorant and subservient.

Locally, the town of Sardis lay about 30 miles from Thyatira. At that time it was one of the richest cities in the world, but money does not buy everything, and it certainly does not buy peace, enjoyment or salvation. The name 'Sardis' means 'escaping ones' and that is very appropriate for those who escaped from Romanism. There are millions today who need the same escape. Sadly, in escaping from Romanism, many of these early Reformers founded their own sects or denominations, so Protestantism was divided and still is. Isn't it true today that people say 'I am a Presbyterian . . . a Baptist . . . a Pentecostal . . . a Methodist' or something else? These titles should not be necessary. When we preach the Word of God we invite people to become *Christians*. They need to be saved! They need to become believers! Is there someone reading this with that need today? Then, my friend, repent of all you sin, and ask the Lord Jesus Christ to save you. 'Behold, I stand at the door and knock.' Do you hear that knock, friend? Listen to His promise: 'If any man hear My voice, and open the door, I will come in to him.' Use the words of the old chorus:-

> Into my heart, into my heart,
> Come into my heart, Lord Jesus;
> Come in today come in to stay,
> Come into my heart, Lord Jesus.

The people in Sardis had a name, but the Lord saw that in many cases it was only *formal*. In chapter 3:4 He mentions that 'Thou hast a few names even in Sardis which have not defiled their garments; and they shall walk with Me in white: for they are worthy.' There was only a very small number of true and faithful people there. Is that the situation here today?

'Behold, I stand at the door and knock.' Let us look next at Philadelphia:-

A FRUITFUL CHURCH

The name Philadelphia means 'brotherly love' and in this Church period which ran from around 1750 to the 1900s it certainly was most *fruitful*. This was the period of great evangelism. This was a time of Christian love when the Lord raised up great preachers, such as DL Moody, CH Spurgeon, John Wesley, Charles Finney, George Whitefield and many others. Great missionaries too such as David Livingstone, CT Studd, Hudson Taylor and others pioneered the world with the true gospel.

The city of Philadelphia was about 30 miles from Sardis. Revelation 3:8 states 'I have set before thee an open door, and no man can shut it.' This 'open door' was obviously a challenge to go out with the gospel and evangelise. Today, we too need to do the same. The Lord's last command to His followers was 'Go ye into all the world, and preach the gospel to every creature' (Mark 16:15). Are the Lord's people doing that today? Is He perhaps calling someone *now*? Is the Lord Jesus Christ knocking and saying to some person reading this 'YOU GO'? The need today is truly colossal. Millions are going to hell without a Saviour. As the words of the hymn remind us, we need to:-

Tell the whole wide world of Jesus,
Bear the news from shore to shore;
Telling sinners of the Saviour,
Let the light spread more and more.

The seventh and last church is Laodicea. It was:-

A FRIGHTFUL CHURCH

Laodicea was a wealthy business city 45 miles from Philadelphia. It was a centre of commerce and finance. It was a place of theatres, shopping centres, lavish baths and a great stadium. The church here was worldly, wealthy, wretched, weak and mostly without Christ. Does that not describe the church of today? We are living in the Laodicean Period of Church history. All around us we can see places of worship which once were alive with the gospel. Now they are religious entertainment centres. Good, old-fashioned preaching of sin and salvation, heaven and hell, are being replaced with bands, pop gospel music, charismatic shows or a bloodless gospel. Is it any wonder then that the Lord speaks of spewing this church out of His mouth? Today's church makes the Lord sick. Too many places of worship are just playing at things. The Lord Jesus Christ is *outside.* We have today a 'No-Saviour gospel.' And people are going to hell as a result. Committees, clubs and social activities need to go. Today's church needs to get down on its knees and pray. We need the preaching of Repentance and Salvation. The Lord Jesus is saying again to this church: 'Behold, I stand at the door and knock.' This church truly is *frightful.*

As the Bible indicates that this Age of Grace will end with this frightful church, we ourselves who know and love the Lord ought to show ourselves as different. We need to leave any apostate church. We need to pray. We need to seek the lost. And, thankfully, the Lord has promised that if we open the door He will be with us. His word is 'I will never leave thee, nor forsake thee' (Hebrews 13:5).

As we close, is there perhaps someone reading this who is unsaved, and needs to open their heart's door? Jesus is knocking. He is waiting to save you now.

> Behold Me standing at the door,
> And hear Me pleading evermore;
> Say, weary heart, oppressed with sin,
> May I come in? May I come in?

CHAPTER THREE
COME UP HITHER

Reading: Revelation 3:14 to 4:5

Text: Revelation 4:1: 'Come up hither.'

INTRODUCTION

The Book of Revelation is one of the most thrilling books in the Bible. Yet to many it is a closed book, for they do not understand it. Revelation is in three parts – as John mentions in Chapter 1:19. It deals with 'the things which thou hast seen, and the things which are, and the things which shall be hereafter.' The Past – what he had seen in his vision on Patmos – is dealt with in chapter 1. The Present – that is the whole era of the Church – is dealt with in a panoramic way in chapters 2 and 3. Then, 'the things which shall be hereafter' – the Future – is revealed in chapters 4 to 22.

We live today in the closing days of 'the present' – the Church Age. In Revelation chapters 2 and 3 there are seven churches mentioned. Each of these – Ephesus, Smyrna, Pergamos, Thyatira, Sardis, Philadelphia and Laodicea – was a real place. But each of these churches represents a period in the history of the Church between Pentecost and the Rapture of the Church. Last century was the Philadelphian era – the period of world evangelism. Revelation 3:8 says 'I have set before thee an open door' – and certainly, the last century was the greatest period of evangelism and missionary work since apostolic times.

The recent period has been that of the Laodicean Church. This church is lukewarm and it is disgusting to God. Revelation 3:15,16 says 'I know thy works, that thou art neither cold nor hot; I would thou wert cold or hot. So then because thou art lukewarm, and neither cold nor hot, I will spue thee out of My mouth.' The present-day church is indeed typified by our present-day society – see verse 17 – 'rich and increased with goods and have need of nothing. We live today in such times! They are indeed *The Last Days* of the Age of Grace. The Bible nowhere teaches that this age will end in revival. Rather, it is to end in apostasy! It is to be a wicked time, followed by the world's great period of judgment – the *Great Tribulation*. Before it commences the Lord Jesus Christ is to come for His Own. 'Worse and worse' is the end-time sign! Suddenly one of these days or nights Jesus will come! This is our hope!

Revelation 4:1 says 'After this' – after the Laodicean Age – 'a door was opened in heaven: and the first voice which I heard was as it were of a trumpet talking with me; which said, Come up hither.' This is our text – the last three words – 'Come up hither.' We shall consider it in two ways. Firstly:

THE CALL OF THE BRIDEGROOM

The Lord Jesus Christ presents Himself in the Bible as the heavenly Bridegroom. In Matthew 25, for instance, He told the parable of the ten virgins, and in verse 6 we read 'At midnight there was a cry made, 'Behold the Bridegroom cometh.'' In this parable there were five virgins who were wise and five who were foolish. Five were *saved* - they had 'oil' which is a symbol in the Bible of the Holy Spirit. The other five were religious – but *lost*. They had no oil! They had never been born again of the Holy Spirit. In verse 10 of Matthew 25 we read 'They that were ready went in with Him to the marriage: and the door was shut.'

In Revelation 4:1 we have the call *of the Bridegroom*. 'Come up hither.' Notice firstly there was:-

A DOOR OPENED

The Bible says, 'A door was opened in heaven.' On that day when Jesus comes back for His Own heaven's door will be wide open – open for His Bride – the true Church. A door is something by which we enter a place. We go into houses, churches and buildings through a door, and if we ever hope to get to heaven it must be by *The Door*. The Bible says there is only one Door. The Lord Jesus Christ in John 10:9 says 'I am the door: by Me if any man enter in, he shall be saved.' The Lord Jesus is the *only door* to heaven. As Dr MR DeHaan once said: 'He is the way *into* heaven and the way *out of* the world.'

The door of heaven – the door of salvation – is open today. If you are not saved, then repent of your sin and ask the Lord Jesus Christ to save you. Revelation 3:20 tells His words: 'Behold I stand at the door and knock.' He is waiting to enter *your* heart's door today. Heaven's door is open. The Lord Jesus says 'Come.' Will you respond?

A VOICE HEARD

This is surely the voice of the Bridegroom, saying 'Come' – 'Come up hither.' Do you not remember the words of Jesus saying 'Come unto Me all ye that labour and are heavy laden and I will give you rest' (Matthew 11:28)? Are you seeking for rest, my friend? Do you look for peace? Then listen to the voice of the Saviour saying 'Come.' We meet many people today who are looking for rest and peace in the wrong places – in church, in good deeds, in honesty, in sincerity, in kindness. There is only One Who can give true peace – the Lord Jesus Christ.

A voice heard! John heard that voice, and when the call of the Bridegroom goes forth some day soon, only those who are saved will hear that voice. The world will not hear it. Only those on the right wavelength will hear that voice, and we only get on the right wavelength by trusting the Lord Jesus Christ as our personal Saviour. Friend, are you *saved?* Are you washed in the precious blood of the Lord Jesus Christ? Are your sins forgiven? Do you have peace with God? If you wish to hear the call of the Bridegroom then you must be ready and listening!

THE TRUMPET CALL

Revelation 1:10 says ' I was in the Spirit on the Lord's day, and heard behind me a great voice, as of a trumpet.' This is the voice of the Saviour. From Him goes forth the trumpet call, and the call is this: 'Come up hither.' In 1 Thessalonians 4:13-17 we have Paul's wonderful description of the Rapture of the Church. He says 'I would not have you to be ignorant, brethren, concerning them which are asleep, that ye sorrow not, even as others which have no hope. For if we believe that Jesus died and rose again, even so them also which sleep in Jesus will God bring with Him. For this we say unto you by the word of the Lord, that we which are alive and remain unto the coming of the Lord shall not precede them which are asleep. For the Lord Himself shall descend from heaven with a shout, with the voice of the archangel, and with the trump of God: and the dead in Christ shall rise first: Then we which are alive and remain shall be caught up together with them in the clouds, to meet the Lord in the air: and so shall we ever be with the Lord.'

You must have noticed Paul's reference there to the 'trump of God.' A trumpet always gives a loud, clear call. This trumpet call is *the call of the Bridegroom*. 'Come up hither.' This is His call to His waiting Bride. This is His call to 'Come.' This is His way of saying that the Age of Grace is through and the Marriage Feast – the Marriage Supper of the Lamb – is about to begin.

When that trumpet call goes forth it will then be too late to get saved. The Bible says 'Now is the accepted time, behold now is the day of salvation' (2 Corinthians 6:2). Will you not make sure now that you are ready?

When the trumpet call goes forth no unsaved soul will hear it, but millions of blood-washed souls over the face of the earth will disappear. Some will be sleeping. Some will be working. Some will be travelling. And when the trumpet call sounds, all who are saved by the grace of God will be 'caught up to meet the Lord in the air.' Is this your hope, my friend?

Some day soon, there will be *the call of the Bridegroom* - 'Come up hither.' Now, let us look at the other side:-

THE COMING OF THE BRIDE

Our text says 'Come up hither.' Notice, first of all:-

THE RESPONSE

The call of the Bridegroom will bring a marvellous response from all over the world. From every corner of the globe men and women, boys and girls who have been saved will rise to meet the Lord. From their quiet resting-places all who have died, over the centuries, trusting in Christ as Saviour will 'rise first.' The infallible Word of God says this! And they will meet all the living believers at that great meeting in the air. As the hymn says:-

There's going to be a meeting in the air,

In the sweet, sweet by and by;

I'm going to meet you, meet you over there

In that home beyond the sky;

Such singing you will hear, never heard by mortal ear,

'Twill be glorious, I do declare!

And God's Own Son will be the leading One

At that meeting in the air!

In Revelation 4:1 the apostle John represents the Church. The last Church Age – the Laodicean period – is through, and John says 'After this', and then he hears the call of the Bridegroom 'Come up hither.' This is the call to the Bride of Christ – the True Church. Nowhere in the Bible does it say that people who were christened or baptised, members of the church or partakers of communion will be allowed into heaven. Only those who are washed in the Lamb's precious blood will be there. Are *you* ready, my friend? Are you washed? Are your sins blotted out? If not, what will your response be today? When the call of the Bridegroom goes forth it will be too late to get saved. Do it NOW! Ask the Lord Jesus to save you NOW.

Those of us who are saved are 'Looking for that blessed hope' (Titus 2:13). We are looking for the Saviour and longing for His return.

'Come up hither'. These words will announce the coming of the Bride. Revelation 22:17 says this: 'The Spirit and the bride say, Come.' This is her response. Notice, also, besides the response, there is:-

THE REJOICING

The uniting of the Bride and the Bridegroom will surely be a cause for great rejoicing. For centuries, the Lord's people have longed for His coming. A loving girl, who is engaged, will truly long for her fiancé's return. And, in the midst of earth's troubles and trials, persecution and opposition, we who love the Lord must be longing for His coming. John Peterson has expressed it in these beautiful words:-

> Looking for Jesus, looking and longing,
> Longing my Saviour to see;
> When there before Him, bathed in His glory,
> Oh, what a joy it will be!
> Caught up to heaven, in clouds to meet Him –
> Can it now be far away?
> Hope of the Christian that keeps me expectant
> And looking for Jesus today
> Looking for Jesus each hour that passes,
> For He may come any time –
> Sunrise or sunset, noonday or midnight
> Could be that moment sublime!
> I must be ready, waiting and watching,
> House all in order alway,

Poised for the sound of that heavenly trumpet
And looking for Jesus today!

In 1 Thessalonians 2:19,20 Paul says 'For what is our hope, or joy, or crown of rejoicing? Are not even ye in the presence of our Lord Jesus Christ at His coming? For ye are our glory and joy.' For the great apostle to again be with people he had led to Christ was a cause for rejoicing. To meet the Saviour empty-handed will be tragic! Christian friend, what have *you* done for Him since He saved you? How many souls have you led to Christ? How many opportunities have you missed? There is no greater joy to be found than in bringing people to Jesus.

Look now at Revelation 19:7. 'Let us be glad and rejoice, and give honour to Him; for the marriage of the Lamb is come, and His wife hath made herself ready.' You will notice how the Lamb of God – the Bridegroom – is the One to be honoured. This will be a wonderful day of *rejoicing!*

THE REWARDS

'Come up hither.' These words will announce the coming of the Bride. She makes her *response*. Then, there is *rejoicing,* and finally we have the *rewards.*

In 2 Corinthians 5:10 we read 'We must all appear before the Judgment Seat of Christ. This is where the *Christian* – not the unsaved – will be judged. Paul says 'that every one may receive the things done in his body . . . whether it be good or bad. In Romans 14:12 the Bible says 'Every one of us shall give an account of himself to God.'

Here, the child of God who has been faithful will be given many rewards. Here, also, the Christian who has wasted his time and talents will see his rewards which might have been, going elsewhere. The Bible says 'God is faithful' (1 Corinthians 10:13). *He* will be our Judge. *He* will bestow the rewards. The Bride will come in answer to the Bridegroom's call – as Paul says – 'In a moment, in the twinkling of an eye' (1 Corinthians 15:52).

CONCLUSION

'Come up hither.' We may hear these words at any time now. There is no known prophecy to be fulfilled. Only the Church has to be completed. Any moment the last person to be saved will accept Christ as Saviour, and the Bridegroom will call and immediately the Bride will come!

Are you 'in Christ', my friend? Are you saved? Have you been forgiven? If not, ask the Lord Jesus Christ to save you *now,* while you have the chance. Tomorrow may be too late!

> There is life for a look at the Crucified One.
> There is life at this moment for thee.
> Then look, sinner, look, unto Him and be saved:
> Unto Jesus Who died on the tree.

Will you look – *now* – before we hear these words: 'Come up hither'?

CHAPTER FOUR

THE BOOK OF REDEMPTION

Reading: Revelation 5

Text: Revelation 5:9: 'Thou . . . hast redeemed us to God by Thy blood out of every kindred, and tongue, and people, and nation.'

INTRODUCTION

Revelation chapter 5 follows chapter 4, where the apostle John has been caught up to heaven. He had described the story of the Church in chapters 2 and 3, and his visit to heaven is a picture of the Church being caught up at the Rapture. This event may take place any time now, as we live in the end of the Laodicean period, where the Church of Jesus Christ is totally indifferent and ineffectual. The Bible says the Church is lukewarm. A cool situation is present today. Where do we see Christians on fire for the Lord? Where do we see men and women preaching in the open air, and going from door to door with Gospel tracts? Where do we hear folk in the Prayer Meeting crying to God to save the lost souls of their friends and loved ones? We need a burden today for the lost. When did *you* last invite a friend or someone off the street to come and hear the Gospel? Every born again person should be a seeker of the lost.

Revelation 5 presents a different scene. John is in heaven and he is watching. The matter which takes his notice is:-

THE SEVEN SEALED BOOK

Verse 1 says 'I saw in the right hand of Him that sat on the throne a book written within and on the backside, sealed with seven seals. The Seven Sealed Book. What was it? Those looking on were curious, and so was John. This book was the Title Deed to the whole earth. That Title Deed was lost when Adam sinned. Before then he was in control, but he sinned. He broke God's law and lost everything. Satan took control to a large extent. The Curse fell, and that which was beautiful and lovely became corrupted and sinful. Weeds grew. Animals became wild and the whole creation was affected. In Romans 8:22 we read Paul's words 'The whole creation groaneth and travaileth in pain together until now.' Sin brought suffering. Sin brought disaster, and Satan took full advantage of the situation.

While this is the present case, God promised in His Word that the situation would be changed eventually, and after the Rapture – about seven years later – the Lord is going to restore the earth. Isaiah 35:1 states 'The wilderness and the solitary place shall be glad for them; and the desert shall rejoice, and blossom as the rose, and the parched ground shall become a pool, and the thirsty land springs of water.' That day is coming, but all the Lord's dear people will be away before then. The Lord Jesus Christ is coming again – soon; any time. Are *you* saved? If you are not, it will be too late then to repent and trust Him. Do that *now*, while you may.

That book or scroll is the Title Deed to the earth, and the earth is to be redeemed one day. The curse will be gone. Hundreds of millions of Christ-rejecting sinners will be dead in the Tribulation judgments. When the Lord Jesus Christ went to Calvary, He was wearing a crown of thorns. In Genesis 3 where we learn of Adam's sin, we read about thorns. They never existed before the fall, and our Saviour was crowned with them. He suffered for us, because He 'loved us and gave Himself for us' (Ephesians 5:2).

The Seven Sealed Book is the book of redemption. Notice the words of our text: 'Thou hast redeemed us by Thy blood.' Redemption can only come through someone paying the price, and the Lord Jesus Christ was the only One who could do that for us. They hymn writer penned these lovely words:

Redemption! Oh, wonderful story –

Glad message for you and for me:

That Jesus has purchased our pardon,

And paid all the debt on the tree.

From death unto life He hath brought us

And made us by grace sons of God;

A fountain is opened for sinners:

Oh! wash and be cleansed in the blood.

'Thou hast redeemed us to God by Thy blood out of every kindred, and tongue, and people, and nation.' Are you, my friend, redeemed?

THE SOLEMN SEARCH

Verses 2 and 3 of this chapter of Revelation tell us that a solemn search was made in heaven and earth for someone who could open this Seven Sealed Book – but no one was found. The strong angel asked simply if there was someone worthy – moral and spiritually right, someone who was the rightful heir, someone who had paid the price of redemption. The angels were not qualified. Adam could not do it, for he was the one who disobeyed God and brought the world into judgment. Verse 4 states 'No man was found worthy to open and to read the book, neither to look thereon.' Now, we learn that the apostle John was very upset, for he was most anxious to know the contents of the book. The fact simply was that no man – no human being – could ever be a Redeemer. No sinner can ever pay the price for sin. No one can. And today we live in a world which needs a Redeemer. We, who are saved, know that Redeemer – the Lord Jesus Christ, for He has saved us and redeemed us eternally. As the Bible says, we 'are redeemed . . . with the precious blood of Christ' (1 Peter 1:19).

What does our text say? 'Thou . . . hast redeemed us to God by Thy blood out of every kindred, and tongue, and people and nation.' It is great to be redeemed! Christian friend, do you thank the Lord continually for redeeming you?

The solemn search resulted in no man being found. But, there came good news! One of the elders in heaven turned to John and told him that there was One Person who could open the book, and He was:-

THE SATISFYING SAVIOUR

The Satisfying Saviour. Verses 5 to 7 explain it all. 'The Lion of the tribe of Judah, and Root of David, hath prevailed to open the book, and to loose the seven seals thereof.' The Lord Jesus is the champion. He is the all-victorious One. He can do what others cannot do. He is the Mighty Redeemer – the Redeemer of souls, and also the Redeemer of the earth. He paid the price on Calvary's mountain for poor, lost, hell-deserving sinners. He paid the price of our sin. No man can ever make atonement for sin, but the sinless One, the Lord Jesus Christ, paid our penalty in full. The poet asks the question 'Why?'

> Why did they nail Him to Calvary's tree?
> Why? Tell me why was He there?
> Jesus, the Helper, the Healer, the Friend,
> Why, tell me why was He there?
> All my iniquities on Him were laid,
> He nailed them all to the tree;
> Jesus, the debt of my sin fully paid;
> He paid the ransom for me.

'Thou . . . hast redeemed us to God by Thy blood.' Yes, friend, it was the sinless blood of the Lord Jesus Christ, shed on the Cross at Calvary, which paid the price. He is the great Redeemer. Has He redeemed *you*, friend? If not, then now is the time to repent and ask Him to save you. The Lord Jesus Christ is the Satisfying Saviour. He satisfies me, and He will satisfy you too if you will trust Him.

We find in Revelation 5 that John turned to look at the Lion, but he saw instead a Lamb. This was the One to Whom John the Baptist referred as 'The Lamb of God Which taketh away the sin of the world' (John 1:29). Back in Genesis 3 the earth was cursed when Adam sinned. However, the Lord promised Redemption ultimately. All through the Old Testament era people had to take a lamb which was perfect and make it a sin-offering – looking forward to the eventual coming of the Lamb of God, the Lord Jesus. Today we look back to the Cross where that precious Lamb of God made atonement for our sin. He opened the way for sinners to get right with God. He satisfies every soul who trusts Him savingly. As Kinsman-Redeemer He purchased the Title Deed of the earth, and it will be redeemed when He comes back as King to reign. Meantime, He is saving lost souls and becoming their Redeemer.

Many years ago in one of the Southern States, a 15 year old girl was put up for sale as a slave. The bidding commenced, but one man kept outbidding all the others and eventually he bought her. As they left the sale he asked her quietly if she could read, and she said 'Yes, a little.' The man turned to her and handed her a paper and said 'I don't need you, for I am a millionaire. Here is the parchment making you free. I felt sorry for you standing there looking so sad. You are free to go now.' The man walked off, and the girl ran after him with tears streaming down her cheeks, and she said 'Sir, may I go home with you and work for you?' The man took Jane home to his plantation and there she spent her life working day in and day out for the man who had redeemed her from slavery. Many years later Jane was dying. Her friends gathered around her, and suddenly her master, who was now in his nineties, appeared. And Jane called out once more: 'Thank you for redeeming me and setting me free.' Friend, are *you* satisfied with Jesus? He has purchased our redemption – something we never deserved. He paid the price for us. And, He truly *satisfies* all those who live for Him.

'Thou . . . hast redeemed us to God by Thy blood.' Yes, the blood had to be shed, and it was shed at Calvary – for you, for me. Can you echo the words of the chorus?

> Thank you, Lord, for saving my soul;
> Thank you, Lord, for making me whole;
> Thank you, Lord, for giving to me
> Thy great salvation, so rich and free.

We have looked at the Seven Sealed Book, the Solemn Search and the Satisfying Saviour. Let us, finally, consider:-

THE SONG OF THE SAINTS

Revelation 5:9-14 tells us something of this song. It commences 'They sing a new song, saying, 'Thou are worthy.'' Verse 12 says 'Worthy is the Lamb that was slain to receive power, and riches, and wisdom, and strength, and honour, and glory and blessing.' All the hosts of heaven join in this great song – the elders, the angels and all creation joins in the Song of the Saints.

Singing is something special. People who are miserable and unhappy do not sing. But joyful people do! What the apostle John saw was a foreviewing of what is going to take place. The day is coming when all heaven will sing the praises of the Saviour. Our text says 'Thou hast redeemed us by Thy blood.' What a song! The Song of the Saints will come from grateful hearts. Men and women, boys and girls who have been saved and redeemed eternally will be joined by the angels and all creation in praising the Lamb of God – the Lion of the tribe of Judah – the Lord Jesus Christ. What an occasion that will be! Will *you* be there, my friend? Only saved ones – people who have had the cleansing of the precious, sinless blood of the Saviour – will be there.

Money cannot pay the price for sinners. Good works also are useless. Faith in the finished work of the Lamb of God is what is required. William Cowper penned these words:-

> Dear dying Lamb! Thy precious blood
> Shall never lose its power
> 'Till all the ransomed church of God
> Be saved to sin no more.

We can rejoice that in heaven there will be no sin. The price was paid. 'Thou hast redeemed us to God by Thy blood.' What a word! Christians today ought to rejoice in this verse. We need to remember daily the price that was paid for us on Calvary. But, don't we forget?

The late Sir Harry Lauder told the story of a visit he made to America. There he learned from a friend that American homes which had lost a son in the war were told that they could put a star in their windows of their houses. One night this man was walking along with his wee boy and he explained the meaning of the stars to the lad. Suddenly, the wee fellow exclaimed 'Daddy, God has lost a Son. Look up. He has stars in His window.' Yes, friend. 'God so loved the world, that He gave His only begotten Son that whosoever believeth in Him should not perish but have everlasting life' (John 3:16). What a message!

Will you, friend, be in heaven on that great occasion when the whole company of saints sings that great new song of praise to the Lamb that was slain? 'Thou hast redeemed us to God by Thy blood.'

Some time ago it was my privilege to share in the baptism of a man. He had lived a very wicked life, but a friend gave him a gospel tract and spoke to him. Later, he sought the Lord. His whole life was transformed. He discovered a wonderful hymn, and it became his favourite. The words are these:-

> Come, sing, my soul, and praise the Lord
> Who hath redeemed thee by His blood;
> Delivered thee from chains that bound
> And brought thee to redemption ground.
> Redemption ground, the ground of peace!

Redemption ground, oh, wondrous grace!
Here let our praise to God abound,
Who saves us on redemption ground.

That brother is now in heaven. Will YOU be there? There is only one way: the Lord Jesus Christ. Trust Him now as your Saviour. Then, you will be able to say 'Thou hast redeemed us to God by Thy blood.'

CHAPTER FIVE

THE FOUR HORSEMEN

Reading: Revelation 6

Text: Revelation 6:2: 'Behold a white horse.'

Revelation 6 mystifies many people. What is meant by this chapter? Who are these four horsemen and why are the horses different colours? All prophetic teaching can be difficult to understand if we are not familiar with true prophecy. The apostle John wrote down for our edification all that he was told to, and here in this chapter the Lord gives a bit more information about the period called the Tribulation. These four horses are still future. The Tribulation is also future. It is not far distant, for all the signs in the world today point to the very near return of the Lord Jesus Christ for His Own.

This chapter commences with the Lamb – the Lord Jesus Christ – opening the first of the Seven Seals. John tells us in v. 2: 'Behold a white horse.' These words are our text and they lead us to consider:-

THE WHITE HORSE

'Behold a white horse.' Then, the verse goes on to describe the horseman. He had a bow. He also had a crown. And he went forth to conquer. This is not the same rider as we find in Revelation 19, where we are told emphatically that He is the Lord Jesus Christ and there He is returning in power and great glory to take charge of the affairs on earth for a thousand years. This is a different horseman. We find him mentioned in Revelation 13. He is the Beast out of the sea. He is referred to in Daniel, 2 Thessalonians and other parts of the Bible. He is the Antichrist and he is coming! No one will stop his arrival on the earth's scene. Clarence Larkin describes him in this way: 'This is the picture of a brilliant, strategical and irresistible conqueror whose victories will dazzle the world, and elevate him to a leadership that will place him at the head of the Federates Kingdoms of the Revived Roman Empire.' Friend, we see that federation well under way today in the European Union. Britain needs to get out fast from that unholy alliance. The Bible says he will be holding a bow, but no arrows are mentioned. This indicates that he will appear as a great leader, solving the world's problems. Appearing on the world's stage on a white horse, he may be wishing to pretend that he is Christ, but in reality he is Satan's man – the Antichrist. He is an imposter – no man of peace, as we shall see. This superman will not appear until after all the true Christians have been removed at the Rapture. The Bible makes this clear. In 2 Thessalonians 2:8 it states 'Then (after the Rapture) shall that Wicked be revealed, whom the Lord shall consume with the spirit of His mouth, and shall destroy with the brightness of His coming.' That refers to Revelation 19, of course.

This white horseman will come offering peace and prosperity. Millions will believe him and accept him warmly. He will receive a kind of crown as leader of the revived Roman Empire, and three and a half years later as leader and dictator of the whole world. The world will be deceived, and the Bible says in 2 Thessalonians 2:11 'God shall send them strong delusion, that they should believe a lie.' We live in serious times. Terrible things are ahead for all who are not saved. Daniel refers to this man as 'The prince who is to come' (Daniel 9:26).

The White Horse. Yes, it sounds like peace, but soon the world will find otherwise.

'Behold a white horse.' Let us look now at the second horse.

THE RED HORSE

Revelation 6:4 states 'There went out another horse that was red: and power was given to him that sat thereon to take peace from the earth, and that they should kill one another: and there was given unto him a great sword.' Who is this rider on the Red Horse? The rider on the White Horse was pretending to be the Lord Jesus Christ – the Prince of Peace. However, the Antichrist, when he is a world peace-maker will soon find himself faced with rebellion, fighting and much trouble. Yes, Revelation 13:3 tells us 'All the world wondered after the beast.' Satan is going to give the Antichrist his power, and in the world he will have great authority. People will see in him the possibility of peace, and he will solve many economic problems, but that will quickly pass. His great authority will be backed up by the sword. The Red Horse and its rider will bring death and destruction. This rider is the same person as the rider on the White Horse. He is the Antichrist!

Without the Lord Jesus Christ in control, this world shall never know peace. 1 Thessalonians 5:3 says 'For when they shall say, Peace and safety; then sudden destruction cometh upon them.' What a prospect! War, and millions of deaths – that is the future under the rider on the Red Horse! But Jesus is coming before that happens. Are you His? Are you saved and ready? If not, then now is the time to repent and ask Him to save you. He came to this world for our salvation. Do not ignore Him, for you need Him, friend.

The Red Horse will introduce a period of killing, for the peace-bringer will seek to establish himself over the nations of the revived Roman Empire. When the Lord Jesus Christ comes in the air and removes His blood-washed people, the Holy Spirit also leaves. He is the great Restrainer. Paul explains this in 2 Thessalonians 2:7,8: 'He who now letteth (restrains) will (restrain), until He be taken out of the way. And then shall that Wicked be revealed.' The Beast, the Antichrist, will not be revealed to the world while God's dear saved people are on earth. The Bible makes it so clear that in the Tribulation period millions of unsaved people will perish. There will be wars and fighting until he is finally established as ruler of the whole world after three and a half years.

It is significant to note that *red* is the colour of communism and socialism. Russia, China, North Korea and other places are still communistic. They may be quiet just now, but the Lord Jesus, speaking about the end times in Matthew 24 said 'Ye shall hear of wars and rumours of wars . . . For nation shall rise against nation, and kingdom against kingdom.' Terrorism is now open. Terrorism under the Antichrist will be worldwide.

After World War I man tried to make world peace through the League of Nations. After World War II man established the United Nations. These organisations have not prevented wars. Today, politicians and others are working for the New World Order. The Bilderberger Group and the Illuminati are behind all this. The European Union wishes to establish central government and a European army – all preparing the way for the Beast of Revelation 13: the rider on the Red Horse. Horror lies ahead! If you are not saved, friend, you will see this come to pass. Listen to the words of the old hymn:-

> Oh, the precious gospel story
> How it tells of love to all!
> How the Saviour in compassion
> Died to save us from the Fall;
> How He came to seek the lost ones
> And to bring them to His fold:
> Let us hasten to proclaim it,
> For the story must be told.

Yes, friend, 'God so loved the world, that He gave His only-begotten Son, that whosoever believeth in Him should not perish, but have everlasting life' (John 3:16). People today either have this life, or they do not have it. The Bible says in 1 John 5:12 'He that hath the Son hath life, but he that hath not the Son of God hath not life.' We either have or have not. Which is it?

THE FOUR HORSEMEN

Our text says 'Behold a white horse.' We have seen the White Horse, and we have looked at the Red Horse. This chapter in Revelation goes on to discover:-

THE BLACK HORSE

Revelation 6:5 says 'And I beheld, and lo a black horse, and he that sat on him had a pair of balances in his hand.' A Black Horse! Yes, a White Horse, a Red Horse and now a Black Horse. What does this mean? Why all these different colours? White stands for peace, and red for fighting. Black speaks of darkness. The beast who comes as the great peace-maker will deal violently with all who stand against him. Red speaks of bloodshed, and black tells us that many deaths will follow. The rider on this horse does not have a sword, but he is holding a pair of balances or scales in his hand. The word has done its work. Now there is worldwide famine and hunger. Shortage of food always follows war. Food rationing was worse after World War II than during the war. Famine is going to be the order of the day. In Matthew 24:7 the Lord Jesus Christ foretold 'There shall be famines.' Verse 6 of Revelation 6 explains 'A measure of wheat for a penny, and three measures of barley for a penny.' This word 'penny' refers to a denarius. The denarius was the wage of a man for one day's work. So, in the time of famine in the Tribulation Period, food will be terribly scarce and severely rationed. Black or very dark days lie ahead. The Antichrist will impose very severe restrictions over his kingdom. As it is today, we see the beginnings of this with European legislation. This unlawful body is making laws which over-ride our British laws. Freedom is being rapidly whittled away. Our people are being dictated to, and they are accepting it, so, when the Christians are all gone, those left behind will accept gladly the rule of this creature who promises peace but makes war, and when famine occurs, they will accept his rationing.

The prophet Jeremiah wrote in Lamentations 4:9: 'They that be slain with the sword are better (off) than they that be slain with hunger; for these pine away, stricken through, for want of the fruits of the field.'

Part of the reign of the Antichrist will be marked with *death* through famine and hunger. It will be a very black period in earth's history. The balances or scales indicate food rationing. It will be severe and today's famines will be nothing to compare with what is to come. Do we today know anything of famine? – real, desperate hunger? Not in this country. But, the day is coming when there will be world-wide famine, no doubt as a result of war. The only real famine we have is a famine of the Word of God. Men and women are not hearing much preaching of God's Word today. How we need to be fed on His Word, Christian friend! Do you read the Bible daily? Do you listen to God as He speaks through His Word? Listen to the words of the hymn:-

> How firm a foundation, ye saints of the Lord,
> Is laid for your faith in His excellent Word!
> What more can He say than to you He hath said,
> You who unto Jesus for refuge have fled?

God's Word – the Bible – reveals salvation. It also tells us about the future, and that includes the rider on the Black Horse. Yes, friend, this rider is also the same person – the Antichrist. And, friend, he is not far away. Black days are ahead for all who are not saved. Repent now, my unsaved friend, and ask the Lord Jesus Christ to save you!

There is one more horse and its rider to consider, and it is:-

THE PALE HORSE

Revelation 6:8 states 'Behold, a pale horse: and his name that sat on him was Death, and Hell followed with him.' The Pale Horse looks like a dead body. Death, we read, is followed by Hell or Hades, which is the place where all the unsaved go until their eventual trial at the Great White Throne and their sentence to an eternity in the Lake of Fire. Revelation 21:8 states 'And the fearful, and the unbelieving, and the abominable, and murderers, and whoremongers, and sorcerers, and idolaters, and all liars, shall have their part in the lake which burneth with fire and brimstone: which is the second death.' Are *you* going there, friend? All who are saved will never see that place!

The Pale Horse. Death follows war and famine. It also appears that pestilence will take place. What a scene! What a future! And all this is to establish the Antichrist as world ruler! He basically is the rider on the Pale Horse. His coming to power in the world's scene will bring death and a lost eternity to millions. The false peace will be followed by war, then world famine, and then pestilence and death. A quarter of the world's population will die! God refers to this in Ezekiel 14:21 as 'My four sore judgments.'

The coming Antichrist is the opposite of the Lord Jesus Christ. He brings *death* whereas the Lord brings *life*. Jesus said 'I am come that they might have life' (John 10:10). He said in John 14:6 'I am the life.' Have you got this life? If not, you can have it NOW if you wish. 'Believe on the Lord Jesus Christ, and thou shalt be saved' (Acts 16:31).

These terrible days will only be 'the beginning of sorrows' (Matthew 24:8). Many worse disasters will follow in the next three and a half years as God pours out His punishments or judgments on the earth. The Book of Revelation goes on to tell us a lot more. But, will man repent and believe? The answer is NO. Revelation 6 finishes with verses 15-17 where we learn that people all over the world will cry 'to the mountains and rocks, Fall on us, and hide us from the face of Him that sitteth on the throne and from the wrath of the Lamb.' Man will still be unrepentant. Amos 5:18 warns 'The day of the Lord is darkness and not light.'

The Pale Horse speaks of *death* – eternal death! There will not be one Christian here, thank God!

CONCLUSION

'Behold a white horse.' The white horse for the child of God is spoken in Revelation 19, where the Lord Jesus Christ returns after the Tribulation Period to rule over the whole world for a thousand years. Chapter 6 has shown us four horses – all with the same rider, and he is the coming imposter – the Antichrist. He comes on a WHITE HORSE – waving the peace flag. Then, he is on a RED HORSE bringing war. Next, he is on a BLACK HORSE indicating famine and trouble. Finally, he appears on a PALE HORSE, showing the world DEATH.

Today we offer LIFE – great life, eternal life – to all who will repent and be washed in the blood of the Lamb. The Lord Jesus Christ went to the Cross to pay the price of our sin. Will *you* not repent now, friend, and ask Him to save you? The Bible says 'Whosoever shall call on the name of the Lord shall be saved' (Acts 2:21). Will you call now? Today, not tomorrow, is the day of salvation! How will you answer this question?

>Where will you spend eternity?
>This question comes to you and me!
>Tell me, what shall your answer be?
>Where will YOU spend eternity

CHAPTER SIX

THE GREAT TRIBULATION

Reading: Matthew 24:3-30

Text: Revelation 6:17: 'For the great day of His wrath is come.'

INTRODUCTION

We are living in the very end time of the Age of Grace. Christians should look up, knowing that our 'redemption draweth nigh.' The unsaved should beware, for they are in terrible danger, for very soon the worst period of earth's history will be here. Ordinary people in the world fear a nuclear war. The child of God should not fear this for we firmly believe that we shall all be away to glory before such a war breaks out. Jesus is coming! Are you ready? Are you saved, and trusting in Him for the future. If not, then you ought to get ready NOW. The Bible says 'Now is the day of salvation' (2 Corinthians 6:2). Not tomorrow, friend, but NOW!

Days of great tribulation are coming, and nothing can stop the tragedy which will strike this old world of ours. God has planned it, and His will shall come to pass. There is a day soon coming when men and women all over the world will cry out 'The great day of His wrath is come.' Yes, the Great Tribulation is fast approaching!

You may be asking what we mean by the Great Tribulation. Well, the Lord Jesus in Matthew 24:21 said 'then shall be great tribulation, such as was not since the beginning of the world to this time, no, nor ever shall be.' So, we find that it is to be a terrible time – worse than the days of Noah and the Flood, and worse than anything we can imagine. But, the Christian will not be here, for 'the coming of the Lord draweth nigh' (James 5:8). We have a blessed hope – the return of the Lord Jesus for His Own *before* the Great Tribulation begins. Some of the Lord's people have the idea that the Saved will go through the period of the Great Tribulation, and some even think we are in it now. But the Word of God clearly states to the believing Church in Revelation 3:10 'I will keep thee from the hour of temptation (testing) which shall come upon all the world, to try them that dwell upon the earth.' Jeremiah 30:7 says 'Alas! for that day is great, so that none is like it: it is even the time of Jacob's trouble, but he shall be saved out of it.' There you see that the Great Tribulation affects Israel, not the Church! The Tribulation period is seven years long. The Lord Jesus Christ gave a brief description of the Great Tribulation in part of our Bible Reading, in Matthew 24, and we shall now look at those days which lie ahead – the days called in the Bible The Great Tribulation.

DAYS OF DECEPTION

In Matthew 24:4,5 Jesus said 'Take heed that no man deceive you. For many shall come in my name, saying, I am Christ; and shall deceive many.' The Great Tribulation concerns in the main Israel. She will be then looking desperately for her Messiah, and they will be deceived. The Antichrist – the Man of Sin – will be ruling the world and he will have made a treaty with Israel, but at the beginning of the Great Tribulation – at the beginning of the second three and a half year period – he will break this treaty and will set himself up as God to be worshipped.

The Tribulation Period will be divided equally into two three and a half year periods. Daniel 9:27 states how the Antichrist 'shall confirm the covenant (with the Jews) with many for one week (of years); and in the midst of the week he shall cause the sacrifice and the oblation to cease.' Revelation 11:3 says 'I will give power unto My two witnesses, and they shall prophesy a thousand two hundred and threescore days' (three and a half years). The Antichrist will be the chief deceiver, but there will be many deceivers in that period. We see it even today in all the false cults and sects and the host of false religions. But, it will be much worse during the Great Tribulation!

Have you perhaps been deceived by Satan into believing that you are all right as you are? Unless you have come to the Lord Jesus Christ in repentance and asked Him to cleanse you with His precious shed blood, then you are LOST. You have been deceived! Will you not say with the hymn writer:-

Lord, help my unbelief!

Give me the peace of faith,

To rest with childlike trust

On what Thy gospel saith,

That 'Whosoever will believe,

Shall everlasting life receive!

You can have that life – NOW – for the asking! Remember our text says 'For the great day of His wrath is come.'

Secondly, our text speaks of:-

DAYS OF DISASTER

The Great Tribulation – the second three and a half year period, which is what we are really dealing with here – will be a period of great disaster. There are Days of Disaster right ahead – and when the Church has been taken out of the world at the Rapture, those left behind can only look for a time of *disaster* – of killing, of sadness, of terrible unhappiness. The verses before our text speak for themselves. Revelation 6:15,16 say 'The kings of the earth, and the great men, and the rich men, and the chief captains, and the mighty men, and every bondman, and every free man, hid themselves in the dens and in the rocks of the mountains; And said to the mountains and rocks, Fall on us, and hide us from the face of Him that sitteth on the throne, and from the wrath of the Lamb.'

Quite a number of chapters in the book of Revelation are devoted to this matter – the Great Tribulation period, and the judgments of God which will fall in that three and a half year period.

One great disaster will be the world ruler – the Antichrist or Man of Sin; Satan's arch-representative and helper. During the first three and a half years he will come to power in Europe and then his power will spread until he controls the whole earth.

In Matthew 24:7 the Lord Jesus Christ says 'Nation shall rise against nation, and kingdom against kingdom: and there shall be famines, and pestilences, and earthquakes, in divers places.' God will not let this evil personage rule the world without sending many supernatural judgments. Those who worship and follow the beast will, as John says in Revelation 14:10 'drink of the wine of the wrath of God.' The Bible describes the Great Tribulation as a period of darkness, judgment, pain, suffering, woe, warfare, bloodshed, wrath and death. It is no pretty picture! It will be awful to be alive then! Make sure NOW, friend, that you are saved!

'For the great day of His wrath is come.' Yes, friend, God's wrath and judgments are going to be poured out on the earth in such a way that hundreds of millions will die. These are referred to as the Trumpet judgments in Revelation. In the first of these, there is hail and fire mingled with blood cast upon the earth, and a third of the trees and all grass is burned up. The second trumpet sounds, and a great mountain like a volcano erupts into the sea. A third part of the sea then becomes blood. Revelation 8:9 says 'The third part of the creatures which were in the sea, and had life, died; and the third part of the ships were destroyed.' Then, the third trumpet sounds, and John sees in Revelation 8:10 and 11 how a great burning star fell from heaven and this polluted the water supplies. The fourth trumpet causes the third part of the sun, moon and stars to be darkened. Supernatural darkness will terrify mankind. The fifth trumpet sounds and an enormous number of locusts shaped like horses comes out of the earth. In reality they are demons from the pit taking their orders from Satan. These demons will torment mankind for five months, taking their orders from the devil. Things will be so bad that these Days of Disaster will cause men to wish to die. Revelation 9:6 says 'And in those days men shall seek death, and shall not find it; and shall desire to die, and death shall flee from them.'

I am glad I shall not be here! What about you? Will you not ask the Lord to save you NOW?

The sixth trumpet sounds and we see an army of 200 million men riding on horses. These hordes from Satan will kill and destroy all over the world. Revelation 9:18 says 'By these three (fire, smoke and brimstone) was the third part of men killed. Imagine a third of the world's population killed in this judgment! *And it is going to happen!* Christian friend, are you not concerned for your unsaved loved ones and friends who are going to face this? Won't you pray for them, and witness to them that Jesus is coming and soon it will be too late? Today is the day of salvation – tomorrow could be too late! Repent, my friend, and trust Jesus NOW as YOUR Saviour. Jesus is coming, and He is coming SOON!

Dr DeHaan tells of the coming army of 200 million and says 'Just before the return of the Lord in glory there will be the greatest concentration of military power the world has ever seen, under the leadership of two fierce dictators: the political head (the first beast of Revelation 13) and the religious dictator (the second beast of Revelation 13). This army is being prepared in the middle of the Tribulation Period.'

The sounding of the seventh trumpet heralds the closing stages of the Great Tribulation. Then begin the seven vial or bowl judgments and it all culminates in the world's greatest battle at Armageddon. At that point the Lord Jesus returns in power and great glory to defeat the armies and set up His kingdom.

Days of Disaster are ahead for all who are not saved. Do you anticipate them with joy and gladness? Repent now and ask the Lord to save you while

He may. Remember that Jesus said 'Him that cometh to Me I will in no wise cast out' (John 6:37).

Our text reminds us 'The great day of His wrath is come.' We look now at our next thought:-

DAYS OF DEATH

Death, you say! Yes, there will be the world's most terrible carnage during that very short period known as the Great Tribulation. More people will die then than at any other time in the earth's whole history. Man today has the terrible power of death and destruction in his hand. He could wipe out this planet with a few hydrogen bombs, but God has other plans. So, we need not fear this sort of war. However, during the Tribulation much killing will take place.

In Revelation 6 we have the opening of six of the seven seals. These portray *judgment*. The first seal shows the Antichrist going forth as ruler during the Tribulation. The second seal tells of death and trouble ahead. Revelation 6:4 says 'Power was given to him that sat on the horse to take peace from the earth, and that they should kill one another.' Killing goes on all the time, so we can foresee a GREAT time of killing – Days of Death are ahead!

The opening of the third seal tells of the famine that will follow the killing time. When the fourth seal is opened we find in verse 8 'Behold a pale horse: and his name that sat on him was Death, and Hell followed with him. And power was given unto them over the fourth part of the earth, to kill with sword, and with hunger, and with death, and with the beasts of the earth.' A quarter of the earth's population will die under this judgment! The end is getting near. Your only hope, my friend, is to get to know the Saviour, the Lord Jesus Christ. Accept Him at once, while you may, and you will get to heaven with all of us who are saved BEFORE THIS HAPPENS!

Under the sixth Trumpet Judgment we find that another huge death-toll is still to come. Revelation 9:13-21 describes the terrible demonic army of 200 million creatures and in verse 18 we read 'By these three was the third part of men killed, by fire, and by the smoke, and by the brimstone, which issued out of their mouths.' So we find a quarter of the world's population killed in chapter 6 and a third of the remainder killed in chapter 9! Half of the whole population will be killed in the Great Tribulation period. That is besides others who will die from famine, disease and other things.

Days of Death! Is that a happy prospect? Will you be one of those to perish in the Tribulation judgments? You can make sure NOW that you will not, by trusting the Lord Jesus Christ as your personal Saviour. I urge you NOW to repent of your sin and ask for the cleansing of His precious blood.

>What can wash away my stain?
>Nothing but the blood of Jesus!
>What can make me whole again?
>Nothing but the blood of Jesus!

Our text reminds us: 'For the great day of His wrath is come.' My friend, it is coming SOON, but thank God, Jesus is coming for His Own first. Are you ready?

DAYS OF DELIVERANCE

Fourthly and finally, we have Days of Deliverance. Yes, Days of Deliverance for some people will come! Up till now Israel has not come to know her Messiah and Redeemer, but during the Tribulation period they will discover Who He is, and on His return as King of kings they will welcome Him.

In Revelation 7 we find before the seventh Seal is opened that the Lord is going to keep and protect His ancient, earthly people. Verse 3 of chapter 7 says how a great angel cries out 'Hurt not the earth, neither the sea, nor the trees, till we have sealed the servants of our God in their foreheads.' Then we learn that twelve thousand from each of the twelve tribes of Israel will be specially sealed so that no harm can come to them. These 144,000 will become God's special evangelists and missionaries throughout the Great Tribulation. As a result of their preaching a *vast number* will be saved. As verse 9 says 'A great multitude, which no man could number, of all nations, and kindreds, and people, and tongues.' These saved people will be people who never clearly heard or understood the Gospel in the Age of Grace. Those who are here today and know what it means to be 'saved' will have no chance whatsoever of being saved after the Rapture! There is no such thing in the Bible as a second chance. 'Now is the day of salvation!' (2 Corinthians 6:2). All who hear the Gospel now and turn away rejecting the Lord Jesus will perish – perhaps in the Great Tribulation – and go to hell eventually.

Days of Deliverance. Yes, there will be true deliverance for all then who trust the Saviour, but most of them will be executed for their faith. In chapter 7:14 we read 'These are they which came out of great tribulation (margin: 'The Great Tribulation'), and have washed their robes, and made them white in the blood of the Lamb.' The Antichrist and the False Prophet will be demanding worship during the second three and a half years of the Great Tribulation, and all who refuse the mark of the Beast will be executed or beheaded. This will include all the believers that they can find. Thank God, I will not be here then. Will YOU?

By inference, we learn that the believers will be hungry and thirsty. Verses 16 and 17 of chapter 7 say 'They shall hunger no more, neither thirst any more; neither shall the sun light on them, nor any heat. For the Lamb which is in the midst of the throne shall feed them, and shall lead them unto living fountains of waters: and God shall wipe away all tears from their eyes.' To be a Christian then will cost a terrible price. It will truly be a Day of Deliverance when many shall be saved, but the price they will pay will be terrible. Sorrow and sadness and death will be their lot.

CONCLUSION

In this short chapter, we have only skimmed over some of the details of the Great Tribulation. Yes, it is soon to come to pass. The Bible says so, and all the present-day signs point to the Lord's soon coming for His Own. Immediately after the Rapture, the Great Tribulation period will commence. Will YOU be here, or with us in the air? Will you be left behind to face the terrors of the Great Tribulation with all its killings and its martyrdoms? You don't need to be, but if you do not repent now and accept the cleansing of the precious blood of Jesus, you will. And then, even if you remember our warning today, it will be too late to get saved. Your opportunity is NOW.

The child of God has nothing to fear! In 1 Thessalonians 1:10 we read that the Lord Jesus has 'delivered us from the wrath to come.' We will definitely not be here for the Great Tribulation. Romans 8:1 says 'There is therefore now no condemnation to them which are in Christ Jesus.' Are you 'in Christ' or out of Christ?

> One there is Who loves thee, waiting still for thee/
> Canst thou yet reject Him? None so kind as He!
> Do not grieve Him longer: come and trust Him now!
> He has waited all thy days: why waitest thou?
> Jesus still is waiting: sinner, why delay?
> To His arms of mercy, rise and haste away!
> Only come believing, He will save thee now!
> He is waiting at the door: why waitest thou?

Will you ask Him in? – NOW. 'Believe on the Lord Jesus Christ and thou shalt be saved' (Acts 16:31).

CHAPTER SEVEN

THE 144,000

Reading: Revelation 7

Text: Revelation 7:4: 'And there were sealed an hundred and forty and four thousand of all the tribes of the children of Israel.'

INTRODUCTION

Revelation 7 deals with the coming Great Tribulation. The Tribulation Period follows the Rapture of the Church – that glad moment when the Lord Jesus Christ returns to the air and takes away from this wicked world all who are saved. The Tribulation Period lasts for seven years, and the second half is known as the Great Tribulation, for it is during that time that the Lord will pour out on the world devastating judgments. Revelation 6 to part of chapter 19 deals with the Tribulation, and what is going to happen.

When the Rapture takes place, there will not be one Christian left on the earth, but God has His Own plans and He will not allow Himself to be forgotten. The heavenly people – the true Church – will be gone and then the Lord will resume His work with His earthly people, Israel. He is going to separate out 144,000 men of Israel to be His special Tribulation evangelists. Our text states 'There were sealed an hundred and forty and four thousand of all the tribes of the children of Israel.' Here, we are introduced to:-

GOD'S SERVANTS

These 144,000 men are to be God's special servants during the Great Tribulation. The Bible says there will be twelve thousand from each of the twelve tribes of Israel. There are certain Bible students today who imagine that ten of the tribes are missing, but Israel has been scattered around the world for centuries and the Israeli people still keep their identity. There are several million in Israel today, but millions more scattered around the earth. The Lord is going to have twelve thousand from each tribe to be His servant to preach the Gospel of the Kingdom. You may ask what this is. Is it different from the gospel we proclaim today? The answer is 'Yes.' John the Baptist preached the Gospel of the Kingdom. The disciples of the Lord Jesus proclaimed the Gospel of the Kingdom. However, from the Day of Pentecost the message changed, and became the Gospel of the grace of God. That is our message today. Repent, and ask the Lord Jesus Christ to come into your heart and cleanse you with His precious blood! 'Believe on the Lord Jesus Christ, and thou shalt be saved' (Acts 16:31).

God's servants will preach the Gospel of the Kingdom. This message differs from ours because the kingdom is earthly, while the Church is heavenly. All who are saved today are going to heaven. We form part of the Bride of Christ and we shall be with Him for all eternity. The Gospel of the Kingdom concerns the earthly rule of the Lord. That will take place in the Millennium. John the Baptist preached 'Repent ye: for the kingdom of heaven is at hand' (Matthew 3:2). If the Jewish people had welcomed the Lord Jesus Christ, that kingdom might have come, but the Bible says in John 1:11 'He came unto His Own, and His Own received Him not.' Verse 12 however states 'But as many as received Him, to them gave He power to become the sons of God, even to them that believe on His name.' Can I ask you, friend, have YOU believed? Are you saved? Today people can receive the Lord as their Saviour, but the majority reject Him or are totally indifferent. Where do you stand? Is He your Saviour? If not, then use the words of the great old hymn:-

I hear Thy welcome voice
That calls me Lord to Thee
For cleansing in Thy precious blood
That flowed on Calvary.
I am coming, Lord!
Coming now to Thee!
Wash me, cleanse me, in the blood
That flowed on Calvary.

The Cross of the Lord Jesus Christ shows His love for us sinners. Repent and be saved NOW.

GOD'S SEAL

Our text states 'There were sealed an hundred and forty and four thousand.' Note that word 'sealed'. It is important. It is something new and it applies only to these 144,000 Jewish evangelists in the Tribulation. God's seal is to be put upon them. We are not told exactly what this seal is, but it is to be something important which will protect them from death during the reign of the coming Antichrist. This seal will be on their foreheads. There will be no Christians left on the earth, but God is going to choose out of all the Israeli people worldwide this group of evangelists to preach His Word during the Tribulation, and the seal on their foreheads is God's seal to protect them and keep them safe. Satan and the Antichrist will seek to attack and destroy Israel, God's earthly people, because His heavenly people – the Church – will have been caught up to meet the Lord in the air. Revelation 14:1 gives us a clue about this seal. It states here 'I looked, and lo, a Lamb stood on the mount Sion, and with Him an hundred and forty and four thousand, having His Father's name written in their foreheads.' So, we know God's seal will have His name in it. These people will be marked out all over the world as God's servants. That seal will keep them safe.

In Revelation 9 we have the fifth trumpet judgment. It describes a star falling on the earth and various fearsome things that will happen. Verse 4 says 'It was commanded them that they should not hurt the grass of the earth, neither any green thing, neither any tree; but only those men which have not the seal of God in their foreheads.' God's seal is to be their protection as well as their mark as servants of the living God. This leads us on to our next thought:-

GOD'S SALVATION

Through the preaching of the 144,000, vast numbers of people who never previously heard the Gospel will be saved. How do we know this? Can we look into the future: The answer is in God's Word. Revelation 7:9,10 says 'I beheld, and, lo, a great multitude, which no man could number, of all nations, and kindreds, and people, and tongues, stood before the throne, and before the Lamb, clothed with white robes, and palms in their hands; And cried with a loud voice, saying, Salvation to our God, which sitteth upon the throne, and to the Lamb.' These are the many millions who will be saved through the preaching of the 144,000. Yes, friend, there will be vast numbers of people who will be saved in the Great Tribulation period, but not one will have heard the message of the Gospel which we proclaim today. There are more people being born now than can be reached with the Gospel. Sadly, a tremendous number of those who will believe and be saved will be executed. The Bible says in Revelation 7:9 'After this I beheld, and, lo, a great multitude, which no man could number, of all nations, and kindreds, and people, and tongues, stood before the throne, and before the Lamb, clothed with white robes, and with palms in their hands.' In verse 14 we are told 'These are they which came out of the great tribulation, and have washed their robes, and made them white in the blood of the Lamb.' These are the men and women, boys and girls, who will repent and be saved in the Great Tribulation and will be beheaded on the orders of the coming Antichrist. Verse 11 tells us that 'God shall wipe away all tears from their eyes.'

Revelation 13:15 says that the False Prophet, or religious leader in the Tribulation Period will 'cause that as many as would not worship the image of the beast should be killed.' God's salvation will be manifested in the Tribulation – despite all the Satanic activity of the Antichrist and the False Prophet. Vast numbers will be saved, and many will perish. This body of believers though will not be part of the Church, for that body will already be complete and will be with Christ in Glory.

God's salvation in the Tribulation will be different. The people will still repent and be converted, and they will also have a place in heaven, but only those who are saved today in the Age of Grace will be part of the Bride of Christ and be with Him for ever and ever. Our Saviour is still saving today. Are YOU saved? Are YOU ready for heaven? If not, then 'Now is the accepted time, behold, now is the day of salvation' (2 Corinthians 6:2). You may say 'I'll wait and take my chance.' The Bible makes it clear that all who hear and understand the Gospel now in the Day of Grace, and who do not repent and trust the Saviour, will have *no further chance.* In fact, the Lord will harden the hearts of all such people when the Church goes at the Rapture. People will realise that they are lost and they will then become harder and harder. Today, friend, is still the Day of Grace. You can still be saved. Repent now and ask for the Lord to save you and cleanse you with His precious blood. 1 John 1:7 says 'The blood of Jesus Christ His Son cleanseth us from all sin.' God's salvation is available today. Will you repent now and be saved?

The 144,000 will preach the Gospel of the Kingdom, for the King is coming. This leads us on to our final thought:-

GOD'S SON

Revelation 7 mentions 'The Lamb.' The Lamb is the Lord Jesus Christ, the only begotten Son of God. He is the Lamb. In John 1, John the Baptist introduces Him to the multitude in verse 29 by saying 'Behold the Lamb of God, which taketh away the sin of the world.' God's Son, the Lord Jesus Christ, came into the world to save sinners. Many times in the Book of Revelation the Lord Jesus is called the Lamb. Chapter 6:16 refers to 'the wrath of the Lamb.' Chapter 14:1 states 'A Lamb stood on the mount Sion, and with Him an hundred and forty four thousand, having His Father's name written in their foreheads.' Chapter 21 speaks of the 'Lamb's wife' (v. 9), namely the true Church – all who are saved today. Chapter 5 describes the Lamb and His book, and in that book is the name of every blood-washed soul. Chapter 20:15 says 'Whoever was not found written in the book of life was cast into the lake of fire.' Listen to the words of the poet:-

> Is your name written there,
> In the Lamb's Book of Life?
> When you leave this old world
> With its sin and its strife,
> Will they find your name there –
> 'Mongst the ransomed of God –
> In the Lamb's Book of Life
> Through the Lamb's precious blood?
>
> (J Danson Smith)

How do you, friend, answer such a question? Is *your* name in that book? Are you saved and trusting fully for eternity in God's Son? Dr Thomas Chalmers, the great Scottish preacher who led the Disruption, on one occasion while preaching the Gospel suddenly threw out his arm and pointed straight at a famous judge who was in the audience, and he cried out 'Judge, God says 'Now.' Satan says 'Some other time.' What do you say?' That judge rose to his feet and with trembling voice declared 'I have resisted the voice of God too long. I have compromised and put off doing what I should already have done, but now I yield myself to God. I say with Him, NOW.' Is there someone reading this who needs to say NOW? Today – not tomorrow – is your opportunity to be saved. It might be the last opportunity you will have. Will you repent and come to the Saviour NOW?

>Jesus for your choice is waiting;
>
>Tarry not! At once decide!
>
>While the Spirit now is striving,
>
>Yield, and seek the Saviour's side.

Remember, there is only one cure for sin – the precious shed blood of the Lord Jesus Christ. The Bible says 'Without shedding of blood, is no remission' (Hebrews 9:22). And the Lord Jesus Christ shed His blood at Calvary, for you and for me. If you repent now you will be saved for all eternity. But if you live on in your sin, you will end in hell, for ever and ever.

The 144,000 will be pointing men, women, boys and girls to the only Person who can save lost souls, and that Person is JESUS. Matthew 1:21 tells how before He was born instructions were given 'Thou shalt call His name JESUS: for He shall save His people from their sins.' And, we may ask: Who are His people? They are those who repent and trust Him as Saviour!

The Bible tells us that 'God is not willing that any should perish, but that all should come to repentance' (2 Peter 3:9). It also says in Romans 5:8 'God commendeth His love toward us, in that, while we were yet sinners, Christ died for us.' God's Word also says 'God so loved the world, that He gave His only begotten Son, that whosoever believeth in Him should not perish but have everlasting life' (John 3:16).

God's Son is my Saviour. Is He yours?

CONCLUSION

The 144,000 are possibly being prepared now for the eventual service of the Lord, although they will not yet be saved. That will not happen until after the Rapture. That great event may take place at any time now, for all the signs in the world point to the very near return of the Lord. One of these days the trumpet will sound through the heavens and all who are saved will hear it and be caught up immediately to meet the Lord in the air. Black, brown, yellow and white people from all over the earth will suddenly vanish – gone for ever! It will be too late then to get down and repent and cry for the Lord to save you! NOW, and not then, is the time. Families will find loved ones missing. Husbands will find their wives gone, and some unsaved wives will find their husbands gone too. Every blood-washed soul will be 'changed in a moment, in the twinkling of an eye' (1 Corinthians 15:52) – gone to be with their Saviour. Do you want to be left, my unsaved friend? Repent NOW and ask the Lord to save you.

> What shall I do with Jesus?
> For time is gliding by;
> What shall I do with Jesus?
> Eternity is nigh!

'Believe on the Lord Jesus, and thou shalt be saved' (Acts 16:31).

CHAPTER EIGHT

SILENCE IN HEAVEN

Reading: Revelation 8

Text: Revelation 8:1: 'There was silence in heaven.'

INTRODUCTION

'There was silence in heaven.' What strange words! What does this mean, and when will it happen? Revelation 8:1 tells us 'When he had opened the seventh seal, there was silence in heaven about the space of half an hour.' The first four seals reveal the coming Antichrist and the results of his coming. First, he appears as a peace maker, but soon he becomes a war-monger. Then follows famine and pestilence, and finally death to millions. The fifth Seal mentions the tribulation saints – those who will be saved through the preaching of the 144,000 Jewish evangelists whom God is going to raise up. The sixth Seal reveals a tremendous earthquake, worldwide darkness and terror all over. Chapter 8 reveals the opening of the seventh Seal, and this introduces the seven Trumpet Judgments. Verse 2 says 'And I saw the seven angels which stood before God; and to them were given seven trumpets.' Revelation also talks of seven Vials. It seems that the opening of the seventh Seal ushers in the period of the seven Trumpet judgments and the outpouring of the seven Vials.

'There was silence in heaven.' What has happened? First of all we have:-

THE SILENCE OF PREPARATION

Yes, the silence of preparation. Preparation for what, you may ask. The twenty four elders are quiet. The angels no longer speak. The whole host in heaven are silent and the silence is almost terrifying. Preparation, yes, friend, preparation for what is about to come on the earth! The judgments of the Great Tribulation (the second three and a half years) are about to begin. Half an hour goes very quickly if things are normal, but when one is on tenterhooks, half an hour seems like ages!

In chapters 4 and 5 heaven resounds with praise and the worship of the Lamb – the Lord Jesus Christ. Now, there is silence – deathly silence – the silence of preparation. 'There was silence in heaven.' Those in heaven knew that the worst days on earth were yet to come. They stood in awe. It was fearsome, and the apostle John saw all this and wrote it down as a warning. The suspense was terrible. This old earth's most terrifying days were about to happen. At the close of the description of the sixth Seal men were hiding in caves and calling on the rocks and mountains to hide them. But all that was a picnic compared with the Judgments that are to come.

Unsaved friend, you have not the faintest idea as to your future if you remain unsaved. Today, you can repent and put your trust for salvation in the One Who left heaven, came to this earth for 33 years, and went to the Cross to take your punishment. 'For God so loved the world that He gave His only begotten Son that whosoever believeth in Him should not perish but have everlasting life' (John 3:16). Do you have this life? Are you saved and ready for the Rapture? If not, get ready now, while you have the opportunity. 'There was silence in heaven.'

Secondly, we have:-

THE SILENCE OF PRAYER

Certain Christians make a lot of noise when they pray in public. They seem to think that the Lord is deaf! But, millions of prayers are silent as they ascend to God from our hearts. Here, in Revelation 8 we find that during this silence in heaven, the prayers of the saints are offered and are received. Verses 3 and 4 state 'Another angel came and stood at the altar, having a golden censer; and there was given unto him much incense, that he should offer it with the prayers of all saints upon the golden alter which was before the throne. And the smoke of the incense, which came with the prayers of the saints, ascended up before God.' Prayer to the Lord is *always* heard. Never give up praying, Christian friend! Never!

Those who are praying appear to be the people who are saved during the Tribulation through the preaching of the 144,000 Jewish evangelists. Many, if not most, will die under the hand of the Antichrist. In Revelation 6:10 we read that they cry out 'How long, O Lord, holy and true, dost Thou not judge and avenge our blood on them that dwell on the earth?' There was silence in heaven as these prayers were heard. When the silence was over, the fire from the altar of God was emptied on the earth and the great judgments began. All this is future, friend. It is going to take place. John was given a peep into the future, for God wants man to know some of what He has planned. It is a warning to all unsaved to get right with God while they may. The Bible says 'Now is the accepted time, behold, now is the day of salvation' (2 Corinthians 6:2). All who hear and understand the Gospel now and reject it will have no chance of being saved in the Tribulation. The silence of prayer. Yes. Pray silently now, and repent of your sin, and ask the Lord to save you and cleanse you with His precious blood.

THE SILENCE BEFORE PUNISHMENT

'There was silence in heaven.' Yes, this silence preceded the Seven Trumpet Judgments. Punishment is most certainly coming on a world that has rejected the Saviour. The Bible says 'Christ Jesus came into the world to save sinners' (1 Timothy 1:15). But, many today do not wish to be saved. They want to go their own way, sinning and defying the Lord. For them, judgment is coming.

During the opening of the Seven Seals hundreds of millions will have perished. Now, the world is in for very serious *punishment*. Revelation chapters 8,9 and 11 deal with the Seven Trumpet judgments. These are all very specific punishments from the Lord, and men will see that they are from Him.

No wonder that 'There was silence in heaven', for the watchers were to see horrific things happening on the earth. The first Trumpet Judgment is given in verse 7. Here we read 'The first angel sounded, and there followed hail and fire mingled with blood, and they were cast upon the earth: and the third part of trees were burnt up, and all green grass was burnt up.' In other words, one third of all vegetation will be destroyed. Imagine the scene – hail and fire from heaven! This will not be like the bush fires which spring up from time to time. No! It will be fire coming down from above, and fire always leaves a trail of devastation. Black burnt out ruins, charred buildings and dead bodies will be seen all over the world. This will not be an isolated incident, but a world-wide judgment! It will be seen as something sent by God, and sadly, men will still not repent and turn to Him.

The second Trumpet will sound, and Revelation 8:8,9 tells us 'As it were a great mountain burning with fire was cast into the sea: and the third part of the sea became blood; and the third part of the creatures which were in the sea, and had life, died; and the third part of the ships were destroyed.' This sounds like a great meteor which the Lord will allow to strike the earth. For years man has been fearing this, as numbers of large meteors pass the earth from time to time, and scientists tell us that if a large one hit the earth the destruction would be unbelievable. Someone may doubt that the sea could turn to blood. Well, turn back to Exodus and you will find that the Lord turned the waters in Egypt to blood.

The Silence before Punishment. Yes! The watchers are to see much more. Trumpet three sounds 'and there fell a great star from heaven, burning as it were a lamp, and it fell upon the third part of the rivers, and upon the fountains of waters; And the name of the star is called Wormwood.' John goes on to tell us that many died as the waters were poisoned. This is another meteoric judgment. It appears that this meteor will probably skim across the surface of part of the earth, turning all the rivers bitter as it travels. This has already happened when certain volcanic eruptions have poisoned the waters and men died.

What a contrast to the Water of Life – Jesus! John 4:14 records the words of the Lord 'Whosoever drinketh of the water that I shall give him shall never thirst: but the water that I shall give him shall be in him a well of water springing up into everlasting life.' Have *you* tasted of this water, friend? If not, then listen to the words of the Lord Jesus Christ: 'If any man thirst, let him come unto Me, and drink' (John 7:37). Are you perhaps thirsting for life, friend? Then, come to the Saviour. He is the only one Who can satisfy.

Thirst drives people silly. They become desperate. You can picture the scene. People all over the place will drink this polluted water and die. People can live for many weeks without food, but water is a must. Can I ask again, friend: Have you drunk of the water of life? Have you repented of your sin and asked the Saviour to cleanse you with His precious blood? If not, then

> Come for a cleansing to Calvary's tide,
> And be washed in the blood of the Lamb.

It is interesting to note that in the various Trumpet Judgments the Lord uses some of the plagues that He sent on Egypt, but this time it will not be located in just one country, but worldwide. In the fourth Trumpet Judgment, the sun, moon and stars are affected. The sun is darkened and so also is the moon. The Lord Jesus Christ foretold this in Luke:21:25-26: 'There shall be signs in the sun, and in the moon, and in the stars; and upon the earth distress of nations, with perplexity; the sea and the waves roaring; men's hearts failing them for fear.' That day is coming friend, under the reign of the Antichrist. It will happen in the second half of the Tribulation Period. Thank God, the Christians will not be here. We shall be in heaven, attending the Judgment Seat of Christ or at the Marriage Supper of the Lamb.

The fifth Trumpet Judgment announces the arrival of a worldwide plague of locusts – sent to hurt the unbelievers for five months. These are not actual locusts but demonic creatures and they are sent to torment the earth-dwellers, but not the Tribulation Saints, or the 144,000 Evangelists. This invasion from the underworld will cause people to wish to die, but somehow God will prevent them from dying. Jeremiah 8:3 tells us 'Death shall be chosen rather than life.' It will be a terrible situation – suicide wanted, but not effected!

The sixth Trumpet sounds! Here we find an army of two hundred million, and as a result one third of the world's remaining population will be killed, this time by fire and brimstone. And despite all this men will still not repent and turn to the Lord. Thank God we are still in the Day of Grace and we can repent and be saved!

The seventh Trumpet sounds to announce the return of the Lord Jesus Christ in power and glory to reign as King of kings and Lord of lords. This is described fully in Revelation 19.

The Silence before Punishment. Yes, the onlookers had a preview of what is coming on a Christ-rejecting world. 'There was silence in heaven.' Was it any wonder?

We have looked at The Silence of Preparation, the Silence of Prayer and the Silence before Punishment. Finally, we must look at:-

THE SILENCE OF PERDITION

'There was silence in heaven.' Yes, but what is Perdition? The dictionary defines it as 'Eternal death and damnation.' In heaven, those onlookers, including the apostle John, see hundreds of millions of men, women, boys and girls, being put into eternity under all the Trumpet Judgments. And where will these people be going? The answer simply is *Perdition*. A lost eternity. The place of eternal death and damnation. Why? Simply because they will not believe the Gospel.

Let us look at what the Bible says about Perdition. In John 17:12 the Lord Jesus states 'None of them is lost, but the son of perdition.' He was referring to His disciples, and only Judas, who was probably a demon in-dwelt man, was headed for perdition. In Philippians 1:28 Paul says to the Lord's follower that we are not to be terrified by our adversaries. They are bound for Perdition – but we are saved! Hallelujah! The next reference is in 2 Thessalonians 2:3 where we read of the Antichrist – 'the son of perdition.' He is bound for hell. In 1 Timothy 6:9 Paul is speaking of those who put money and riches before the Gospel and they will land in 'destruction and perdition.' Hebrew 10:39 says 'We are not of them who draw back unto perdition but of them that believe to the saving of the soul.'

Can I ask here, are YOU saved? If not, then at this present moment you are heading for Perdition. 2 Peter 3:7 tells of the coming day of judgment and Perdition. The last two references are in Revelation 17, 8 and 11, where the Lord says that the Beast – the Antichrist, the Man of Sin – is going to be sent to Perdition for ever and ever.

Is it any wonder then that 'There is silence in heaven'? The onlookers see only judgment and eternal punishment. That is what awaits all who reject the Lord Jesus Christ as Saviour, or are simply indifferent to Him!

Perdition is a place of 'outer darkness' (Matthew 22:13. It is a place of misery, torment and permanent unhappiness. It is the place of everlasting punishment. God sent His only begotten Son into the world to save people from going there. 'There was silence in heaven.' What a sight! How terrifying!

CONCLUSION

May we remind you that all this is yet future. Today is the Day of Salvation. If you will only repent of all your sin and believe in your heart that the Lord Jesus Christ shed His blood for you, and you ask Him to save you now, He will do that. But it is up to you. We cannot save you. Only Christ can! 'Believe on the Lord Jesus Christ, and thou shalt be saved' (Acts 16:31). 'Whosoever shall call on the name of the Lord shall be saved' (Romans 10:13). Why delay? Come now and trust the Lord Jesus as YOUR Saviour.

>Come to the Saviour, make no delay;
>Here in His Word He has shown us the way;
>Here in our midst, He is standing today,
>Tenderly saying 'Come'!

CHAPTER NINE

GOD'S TWO WITNESSES

Reading: Revelation 11:1-12

Text: Revelation 11:3: 'My two witnesses.'

INTRODUCTION

Our chapter is set in the second half of the coming Tribulation Period – that time known as the Great Tribulation. There is coming a seven year period before long, and it is called the Tribulation, and this is just after the Lord Jesus Christ removes His Church – all the saved ones – from the earth. That may happen any time now. There is nothing left to be fulfilled except the saving of certain individuals who will lead to the completion of the Church, the Bride of Christ. One of these days the trumpet will sound and every blood-washed believer will be caught up to meet the Lord Jesus Christ in the air, and then we shall for ever be with Him. After that takes place the coming world dictator – the Antichrist – will be revealed. He is ready and waiting now, but the Bible says in 2 Thessalonians 2:7,8 that he won't be revealed until the Lord's people are away. The European Union want a leader and they will get their dictator and he will be the Antichrist. This is not fantasy, for Daniel talks of him. Paul refers to him. The apostle John speaks of him and all through the Word of God we find the future foretold. The Antichrist is coming. Do you wish to live under his rule, friend? If not, then put your trust in the Lord Jesus Christ and ask Him to save you.

No Christian will be here then, but God is going to raise up His workers, and in our text we note His words: 'My two witnesses.' Who are they? Let us look first of all at:–

THE ARRIVAL OF THE TWO WITNESSES

In the first two verses of Revelation 11, John is told to measure the temple. This is the Temple at Jerusalem, and he is informed that it will be under Gentile rule for forty two months. It is evident from the Word of God that the Antichrist will interrupt the temple worship and set himself up to be worshipped. This is explained in Matthew 24:15-22 and also in 2 Thessalonians 2:3-4. Jerusalem will be trodden down for forty two months and when this commences, the Lord suddenly raises up His two witnesses. Who are they? Well, we know the name of one for sure. He will be Elijah. Malachi 4:5 and 6 tell us 'Behold, I will send you Elijah the prophet before the coming of the great and dreadful day of the Lord.' In Matthew 17:11 the Lord Jesus said 'Elias truly shall first come.' Elijah has to come before the Lord Jesus returns in power and great glory to reign as King of kings and Lord of lords. Elijah is one of the two witnesses. Then, who is the other? Many Bible scholars are not quite certain, but it appears that the other will be Enoch or Moses. Those who favour Enoch base their argument on the fact that the Bible says 'It is appointed unto men once to die' (Hebrews 9:27), and neither Enoch nor Elijah died. Both were raptured – caught up by the Lord, just as all the Christians will be one of these days! Those who think it might be Moses base their belief on Moses representing the Law and Elijah the Prophets, and because these two men appeared on the Mount of Transfiguration with the Saviour.

The arrival of the two witnesses will cause consternation on the earth. The true believers will have been gone for three and a half years, and suddenly the world is reminded that there is a God in heaven who watches over mankind. Is there someone reading this perhaps who has never thought that way? The Lord is indeed interested in every one of us and He knows His

Own. The others He cares about too, for He sent His only begotten Son into the world to save us lost sinners. John 3:17 says 'For God sent not His Son into the world to condemn the world; but that the world through Him might be saved.' Are YOU saved? If not, then now is the time to repent and ask the Lord into your heart. 'Believe on the Lord Jesus Christ, and thou shalt be saved' (Acts 16:31).

Now, notice secondly:-

THE ACTION OF THE TWO WITNESSES

These two witnesses will be here on earth to act on behalf of the Lord. They will witness for Him in the midst of all the blasphemies of the Antichrist and his next in command, the False Prophet. They will shine as beacon lights in all the world's darkness. The Lord says 'I will give power unto My two witnesses, and they shall prophesy a thousand two hundred and threescore days, clothed in sackcloth.' 1262 days is three and a half years. They will be dressed in mourning. They will prophesy. This means they will tell forth the Word of the Lord. A true prophet is not one who foretells the future, but a man of God who proclaims faithfully the Word of the Lord. How many true prophets have we today – men who fearlessly tell out the Word of the Lord? These two witnesses will proclaim a message of repentance and they will be seen and watched worldwide. We have to remember that the Lord is also going to raise up 144,000 Jewish men to evangelise during this same period, but God's two witnesses will be seen and known worldwide – 'My two witnesses'. These two witnesses will be doing all that the Lord tells them to do. They will be His world-known envoys so that people all over the world will still know that there is a God in heaven to fear and obey.

Verse 5 of Revelation 11 tells us that if people attack or try to hurt them 'fire proceedeth out of their mouth, and devoureth their enemies: and if any man will hurt them, he must in this manner be killed.' No one sensible will attack them. Today certain people attack the Lord's servants. They may not be devoured by fire, but they run great risks, for the Lord takes note. The promise to every faithful Christian is this 'The angel of the Lord encampeth round about those that fear Him' (Psalm 34:7).

These two witnesses will be prophets and their actions will be viewed on TV and seen all over the earth, for they will truly be world news.

We have thought of their Arrival, also their Actions. Let us look, thirdly, at:–

THE AUTHORITY OF THE TWO WITNESSES

'My two witnesses.' Yes, they are *His,* and they have *His* authority. These two prophets will be wonderfully powerful. The Bible says 'I will give power unto My two witnesses.' They will have supernatural powers. Zechariah 4 mentions them as 'two olive trees' and the prophet asks who they are. The Lord replies 'These are the two anointed ones, that stand by the Lord of the whole earth.' (v. 14). Revelation 11:6 says 'These have power to shut heaven, that it rain not in the days of their prophecy: and have power over waters to turn them to blood and to smite the earth with all plagues, as often as they will.' Such happenings will be terrifying to the world's inhabitants. Many will ask: What next? This reminds us of 2 Kings 1, where we read how Elijah was attacked by various groups of soldiers and fire consumed them. They were destroyed, and this will happen again and again when God's two witnesses will be attacked. Fire will kill these people. 'Fire proceedeth out of their mouth, and devoureth their enemies.' That will make fascinating pictures for the TV people, and they will be seen worldwide! These two witnesses will be quite immortal until their work is done. Today we live in the Age of Grace, and the Lord's people do not avenge themselves, but the Great Tribulation will be a period of judgment and punishment. Elijah and his companion will be prophets of judgment.

It is possible that in those days there will be a great question: Who is God? Jehovah or Antichrist? The False Prophet, we learn in Revelation 13, will bring down fire from heaven, but God's Two Witnesses will emit fire from their mouths. The Lord calls them 'My two witnesses.' They will be on earth to publicly witness for the Lord. They will proclaim His message of repentance, and with the 144,000 Jewish evangelists proclaiming the Gospel of the Kingdom, many millions will repent and believe. How do we know this? Revelation 7 speaks about the vast numbers who will perish for their faith during the Great Tribulation. And, remember, no one who knows and understands the gospel today will have a chance of repenting then. The Bible makes that clear. Today is the day of salvation. If you are not saved my friend, repent now of your sin and ask the Lord Jesus Christ into your heart and ask Him for the cleansing of His precious blood. He shed that precious, sinless blood for you – for me. Will you not look to Him now for salvation? Today is the time – not tomorrow, not next week, for it might never come. The Lord Jesus Christ came to save. William Cowper discovered this when he penned the words of the great hymn:–

> There is a fountain filled with blood,
> Drawn from Immanuel's veins,
> And sinners plunged beneath that flood
> Lose all their guilty stains.
> The dying thief rejoiced to see
> That fountain in his day;
> And there may I, though vile as he,
> Wash all my sins away.

The Bible makes it very clear that 'Without shedding of blood, there is no remission (forgiveness) (Hebrews 9:22). You need that cleansing, friend, if you are not saved. 'Believe on the Lord Jesus Christ, and thou shalt be saved' (Acts 16:31).

The Lord's two witnesses will exercise their power and authority against all who resist them. They will be heard and seen world-wide. No doubt news bulletins will announce what they have been saying, although they will probably also mock at them. Their authority will be feared, for they will be on earth when God sends the various Tribulation judgments on the earth when hundreds of millions will die. Truly, fearsome and terrifying days are ahead. Do you really want to be here then?

Let us move on a little. We have considered The Arrival of the Two Witnesses, The Action of the Two Witnesses and The Authority of the Two Witnesses. Let us look finally at:-

THE ASCENSION OF THE TWO WITNESSES

The Ascension. Yes. They are going to ascend! The day will come when their 1260 days are up. Their work and witness for the Lord will come to an end. Satan will make war with them, and the two witnesses will be killed. This reminds us that people tried to kill the Lord Jesus Christ when He was alive, but He was safe until He finally fulfilled the purpose for which He came. Sin was atoned for, and He cried with a loud, triumphant voice 'It is finished' (John 19:30). People thought He was, but He was referring to the work of redemption, and that was complete. Later, men tried to kill Paul, but each time he escaped or recovered, until he finally knew that the time of his departure was at hand. God's servants, when they are faithful, are immortal until their work is done. Remember that, Christian friend, if you are fearful at times. Nothing and no one can harm us without His permission.

Revelation 11:7 says 'When they shall have finished their testimony, the beast that ascendeth out of the bottomless pit shall make war against them, and shall overcome them, and kill them.' How sad! But is it? What happens? These two witnesses will have made such an impact all over the world, proclaiming the Lord's message, that people will be stunned. Satan and the Antichrist will finally have got rid of them. The Antichrist will not allow them to be buried. No, their dead bodies will lie publicly in the street in Jerusalem for three and a half days, with the world's press and photographers fussing around. Revelation 11:10 tells us 'They that dwell upon the earth shall rejoice over them and make merry, and shall send gifts one to another; because these two prophets tormented them that dwelt on the earth.' The world will rejoice that they are dead. But wait! Something wonderful happens. Verse 11 tells us 'After three days and a half the Spirit of life from God entered into them, and they stood upon their feet; and great fear fell upon all which saw them.' Dead men alive again? These awful prophets alive? What is happening? So people will ask.

Verse 12 records to us their ascension. Listen to God's Word. 'And they heard a great voice from heaven saying unto them Come up hither. And they ascended up to heaven in a cloud; and their enemies beheld them.'

Picture the scene. These two prophets of God – 'My witnesses' – after lying publicly dead for three and a half days in the street in Jerusalem, suddenly come alive again, and God's voice is heard calling them to ascend to heaven, and all over the world men and women, boys and girls will see this. And to crown it all the Lord causes an earthquake which will kill seven thousand people in Jerusalem, and a tenth part of the city will be destroyed.

The Lord Jesus Christ was raised from the dead, proving that His death was an adequate atonement for sin, and later He ascended publicly from the Mount of Olives to return to His home in heaven. Do you, my friend have a home there? The Bible says in Acts 3:19, 'Repent ye therefore, and be converted, that your sins may be blotted out.' John 3:16 reminds us that God loves us. 'For God so loved the world, that He gave His only begotten Son, that whosoever believeth in Him, should not perish, but have everlasting life.' Will you believe, friend?

> Sinners Jesus will receive;
> Sound this word of grace to all
> Who the heavenly pathway leave,
> All who linger, all who fall!
> Come, and He will give you rest;
> Trust Him, for His word is plain;

He will save the sinfullest

Christ receiveth sinful men.

If you don't come, you will possibly see and hear these two mighty prophets – 'My two witnesses.'

CHAPTER TEN

ISRAEL AND THE DRAGON

Reading: Revelation 12

Text: Revelation 12:12: 'The devil is come down unto you.'

INTRODUCTION

Our text is set in the middle of Revelation 12. It states 'The devil is come down unto you.' Yes, there is most certainly a devil. He was one of heaven's leading beings, but he became jealous and wished to be equal with God – something which could not be tolerated. So, he rebelled and turned against God, and the Bible tells us that a third of the angels went with him. They lost their state, and today they operate as demons. All Satan's angels are demons, but the true Christian should not be afraid, for when we are saved, we can claim the protection of the precious blood of the Lord Jesus. That blood which cleanses sin away, also keeps the believer safe. God the Father sees the true believing person differently from all other people, for He said in His Word 'When I see the blood, I will pass over you' (Exodus 12:13). If this message is new to someone, I would urge you to repent of all your sin and ask the Lord Jesus Christ to save you and cleanse you with His blood. Remember:-

There is a fountain filled with blood,

Drawn from Immanuel's veins;

And sinners plunged beneath that flood

Lose all their guilty stains.

Revelation 12 records for us something which is ahead for this old world of ours. During the coming Tribulation Period many unusual things will take place. All the Christians will have gone at the Rapture. The Antichrist, the Beast, the man of sin will be ruling the revived Roman Empire. The nation of Israel will have had a measure of peace from her Muslim enemies. The apostle John sees a great wonder, and this leads us to our first thought. Here we see:-

THE WOMAN

The Bible says in Revelation 12:1 'There appeared a great wonder in heaven; a woman clothed with the sun.' Who is this woman? Various women are mentioned in the book of Revelation. Jezebel is referred to in chapter 2. She represents all paganism. The scarlet woman in chapter 17 speaks of the Roman Catholic church and the ecumenical church which are going to compose the coming world church. Here , in chapter 12, the woman is the nation Israel. Some people think that this woman is the virgin Mary. Others have said it is the Church, but no. It is quite clear that this woman clothed with the sun is Israel. Clarence Larkin, CI Scofield, Dr DeHaan, Dr Lehman Strauss and all sound Bible scholars agree that this woman is Israel.

If you look back to Genesis 37:9 you will read of the dream of Joseph being told to his family. 'Behold the sun and the moon and the eleven stars made obeisance to me.' Revelation 12:1 refers to the sun, moon and twelve stars. Israel is referred to again and again as a married woman. Israel is God's earthly people. She has not been faithful to the Lord, and God calls her 'an adulterous wife' in Jeremiah 3. She is called a divorced woman in Isaiah 50:1. Revelation 12:5-6 identifies this woman as Israel, for it was Israel where Christ was brought forth. John 1:11 reminds us 'He came unto His Own, but His Own received Him not.' He was born, lived, died and rose again from the dead in Israel, and thank God, He is coming again! Do you know this wonderful Saviour?

ISRAEL AND THE DRAGON

As Joseph was hated by his family and sold into slavery in Egypt, so Israel as a nation was scattered around the world, and she has been hated and disliked for two thousand years and more, but the day of Israel's glory is still to come when her Messiah – the Lord Jesus Christ – returns in power and great glory to reign for a thousand years. Verse 5 of our chapter states that the man child produced by this woman will rule 'all nations with a rod of iron.' This, friend, is Jesus – no one else. And, Revelation 19 confirms this fully. The day is fast approaching when, as Isaac Watts put it:-

> Jesus shall reign where e'r the sun
> Doth his successive journeys run
> His kingdom stretch from shore to shore
> Till moons shall wax and wane no more.

The woman is Israel. Look next at:-

THE WICKED ONE

Our text states 'The devil is come down unto you.' Verse 3 says 'There appeared another wonder in heaven; and behold a great red dragon.' Who is this 'great red dragon'? We find the answer in verse 9: 'That old serpent, called the Devil and Satan.' He is truly the wicked one. He is the dragon which has attacked Israel all down the centuries, even when scattered, but much more so now that Israel is back in her land. Satan knows that Israel is the Lord's earthly people, and since the Church, by the time this happens will be in heaven, he vents his fury on poor little Israel. He hates Israel because out of her came the Saviour, the Lord Jesus Christ. All who trust Him today as their personal Saviour are safe eternally. When the Lord Jesus was on earth, Satan sought to kill him on many occasions. But, He could not be killed, and even when He hung on the Cross at Calvary, making atonement for our sins, He still could not be killed. The Bible says that He yielded up His life. He shed His precious, sinless blood there for you and me. How wonderful!

Back in Genesis 3:15, when Adam sinned and brought condemnation on the human race which would follow, God gave a promise that the Seed of the woman would bruise the head of the serpent. The Lord Jesus Christ – the Seed of the woman – will bruise and utterly destroy the serpent – the wicked one. Yet, today Satan is at large, 'seeking whom he may devour' (1 Peter 5:8). Satan will oppose any true Gospel work. He will seek to undermine any good work for the Lord. He causes divisions amongst the Lord's people. He is indeed the wicked one. Our text tells the truth: 'The devil is come down unto you.'

Let us look at another scene in this chapter. We have seen The Woman, also The Wicked One. Now, in verse 6 we find:-

THE WILDERNESS

Revelation 12:6 states 'The woman fled into the wilderness.' What is happening? The apostle John is seeing the woman Israel fleeing to the wilderness, in his preview of future events. The devil and the Antichrist are after Israel with great fury to destroy her utterly. 'The devil is come down unto you.'

In case anyone is puzzled, let me explain that there is a huge gap between verses 5 and 6. In verse 5 we learn about 'the man child' – the Lord Jesus Christ. But, since Israel rejected Him He went back to heaven. The Bible says 'Her child was caught up unto God, and to His throne.' More than two thousand years have passed since His birth, and now, during the Tribulation, we find 'the woman fled into the wilderness, where she hath a place prepared of God.' This is to be the Lord's special place of protection for many Israeli people. Many bible scholars speculate that this place may be Petra, which is almost impregnable. Some think that the reference to the woman being given two wings of a great eagle in verse 14 may refer to American protection. But, who knows? We simply are not told. All we know is that in the wilderness she will be safe for quite a long time. Verse 15 informs us that Satan will 'cast out of his mouth water as a flood after the woman, that he might cause her to be carried away of the flood.' Then verse 16 goes on to tell us that 'the earth helped the woman, and the earth opened her mouth, and swallowed up the flood.' Satan may be strong, but the Lord is much stronger, and He will protect His ancient people Israel.

Note the words of our text: 'The devil is come down unto you.' His place has been 'the prince of the power of the air', but God is going to cast him out completely. For a vast number of years he has been admitted to the presence of God to accuse the brethren – the Christians – for none of us is perfect. God has listened, but reminded Satan that *all* the sins of His born again people are dealt with. The Lord Jesus Christ did that on the Cross:-

> On Calvary's brow my Saviour died,
>
> 'Twas there my Lord was crucified!
>
> 'Twas on the cross He bled for me,
>
> And purchased there my pardon free.

Can you, friend, say that you are free? If not, repent now and ask the Lord to save you. The Bible says 'Believe on the Lord Jesus Christ, and thou shalt be saved' (Acts 16:31).

The wilderness. Yes, there will be a place somewhere that Israel in a large measure will be safe. Our next thought brings us to:-

THE WAR

'The devil is come down unto you.' Oh yes, Satan and his emissaries are always around, but the day is coming when he will finally be put out of heaven altogether. Verse 9 states 'And the great dragon was cast out, that old serpent, called the Devil, and Satan, which deceived the whole world: he was cast out into the earth, and his angels were cast out with him.' Verses 7 and 8 speak of the war – war in heaven between Satan and the angels of the Lord. Satan is going to be finally defeated, and we know from later in Revelation he will eventually be sent to the lake of fire to be tormented for ever and ever. That place was prepared for him and his followers, but all who do not trust the Saviour are going there too. Revelation 20:15 states, 'Whosoever was not found written in the book of life was cast into the lake of fire.' What book is this? It is the register of every man and woman, boy and girl who has trusted Jesus as their Saviour. Have you done that, my friend?

It is probable that the war finally commences with the Rapture, for every true believer will be caught up to meet the Lord in the air – Satan's seat – and as we pass through with our Saviour and all the resurrected believers also, the devil goes mad, and Michael – God's commander in chief – leads His army of angelic hosts against the Satanic side, defeating Satan and casting him and his followers down to the earth. Michael is seen all through the Bible as the archangel who does battle for the Lord. Daniel 12:1 tells how in the last days Michael will do battle and Satan will be defeated. Michael and his angels will see to it that the heavens are completely cleared of Satan and all his demons. They will live on the earth for a few years until they are eventually sent to the bottomless pit. What a victory!

Today Satan knows his time is short. He seeks to hinder all Gospel work. He seeks to destroy in many different ways. People today are either on Satan's side, or on the Lord's side. There is no neutral position. Where do *you* stand, friend? If you are not saved, then you are on the Devil's side whether you like it or not. Christian, you must stand up for the Lord and be counted – whatever the cost. No price is too great to pay when the Lord Jesus Christ left heaven and all His glory to save us. Today is still the day of salvation when 'Whosoever shall call on the name of the Lord shall be saved' (Romans 10:13).

Satan and his demons will operate on the earth until they are sent to the bottomless pit for a thousand years, during Christ's millennial reign. Then, soon after, they will taste of the final torments in the Lake of Fire. Do you wish to join them? If not, repent now and ask the Lord Jesus to save you.

We have noted our text: 'The devil is come down unto you.' Today he is in the heavenlies – that area between God's heaven and the world. In the middle of the Tribulation he indeed will be sent down to live here.

THE WINNER

Yes, the winner. We already know who will win, but verse 11 of Revelation 12 says 'They overcame him by the blood of the Lamb.' Yes, friend, it is the *blood* shed on Calvary which finally defeated the Devil. If the Lord had not been born miraculously, He would have been born a sinner. But He was born supernaturally. He was provided with sinless blood, and on the Cross He shed that precious blood for you and me. The Bible says in Leviticus 17:11: 'The life of the flesh is in the blood: and I have given it to you upon the altar to make atonement for your souls: for it is the blood that maketh atonement for the soul.' No Lord's Table or Mass altar can make atonement for sin! Our altar is Calvary. That is where the winner won the victory. When the Lord gave us His life, He cried with a loud voice 'Tetelestai' – Finished. He had finished the work of redemption. His redeeming work was done:-

Redemption! Oh wonderful story –
Glad message for you and for me:
That Jesus has purchased our pardon
And paid all the debt on the tree.
Believe it, O sinner, believe it;
Receive the glad message – 'tis true;
Trust now in the crucified Saviour;
Salvation He offers to you.

Will you do that, friend? Now is your opportunity. The Bible says 'Now is the accepted time, behold, now is the day of salvation' (2 Corinthians 6:2).

CHAPTER ELEVEN
THE TWO BEASTS

Reading: Revelation 13

INTRODUCTION

Revelation 13 tells of the arrival of two beasts or beastly men who are to come to great prominence in this world of ours. The time is future, but not far ahead. Nothing will stop their arrival, for God has revealed it in His Word. The apostle John was given a preview of the events that are to happen, and this coming of the two beasts was one item.

In a day not far ahead – in fact, at any moment – the Lord Jesus Christ will come to the air and the trumpet will sound and all who are saved will hear it and be caught up instantly to meet their Saviour. When that happens there will not be one true Christian left on the earth, and things will go wild. Many will panic at the sudden disappearance of millions, but vast numbers will rejoice that at last they are free to live as they like. This chapter in Revelation describes a trinity of evil which will soon be revealed. Most of us are aware of the Holy Trinity – Father, Son and Holy Spirit. Well, this chapter announces the revelation on earth of a trinity of evil. First of all we find:-

THE DRAGON

Verse 4 states 'They worshipped the dragon.' Who is this dragon? In the previous chapter we find a great battle takes place in heaven between the Lord's army under the archangel Michael and Satan. Satan is heavily defeated and cast down to the earth, along with his hordes of demon followers. He is the Dragon. Satan - no one else! And, before long, people around the world will worship Satan, the Dragon. Today, people know that we ought to worship the one true God, but already Satan is preparing the way with all sorts of false gods, such as Krishna, Buddha, Mohammed, Allah and others. When all of us who preach God's Word and teach that salvation is only through the Lord Jesus Christ have gone, there will be a kind of religious vacuum, and people will start openly worshipping Satan. Satanists today will come out in the open, and as the Bible says 'They worshipped the dragon.' Many people today are involved in spiritism which simply is demon worship. The occult deals with the devil, and no child of God should ever have anything to do with it.

The dragon will seek to control the whole earth and through the other two members of the evil trinity, they will have much success for three and a half years. This period of time is the second half of the Tribulation Period, which is a seven year term beginning after the Rapture of all the believers. Can I ask here: Are *you* saved? Will you, my friend, be caught up to meet the Lord Jesus when He comes to the air? This is something which affects saved people only. Paul, writing to the Christians in Corinth says 'We shall not all sleep, but we shall all be changed; in a moment, in the twinkling of an eye' (1 Corinthians 15:51-52). All the rest of the world's population will remain behind, not knowing what has happened. Soon after, the dragon and his associates will be revealed. Do you fancy living in that day, friend? If not, repent now of all your sin and ask the Lord to save you. Remember, 'The blood of Jesus Christ, His Son cleanseth us from all sin' (1 John 1:7). No sin is too great except the sin of ignoring the Lord Jesus.

>'Tis a true and faithful saying,
>Jesus died for sinful men;
>Though we've told the story often,
>We must tell it o'er again.

THE TWO BEASTS

He has made a full atonement,
Now His saving work is done;
He has satisfied the Father
Who accepts us in His Son.

The Dragon. Yes! Notice, secondly:-

THE DICTATOR

Here, in verse 1, we find a beast rising out of the sea. This is the coming dictator which the world awaits today. Things are so out of hand, both nationally and internationally, that the dictator will be welcomed with open arms. Daniel tells us quite a lot about this dictator. In chapter 7:7,8 he describes something of him with his seven heads and ten horns. It seems from God's Word that he will be ruling the former Roman Empire, namely Europe, and halfway through the Tribulation he will be so energised by the devil that he will become dictator of the whole world for the last three and a half years. This period of time is mentioned both in Daniel and Revelation. This dictator is a man yet to be revealed. 2 Thessalonians 2 indicates that he will not be revealed until all the Christians have gone to be with the Lord. Today the European Union is wanting a president, a dictator or superman to take control. This has been talked about for many years. This beast, the coming dictator, has been called by many names in the Bible. In Isaiah 10:5,6 he is called 'The Assyrian.' In Isaiah 14:4 He is referred to as 'King of Babylon', and in Daniel chapters 7 and 8 he is described as 'The little horn.' Daniel also gives him other titles – 'The king of fierce countenance', 'The prince that shall come' and 'The wilful king.' In the New Testament, in 2 Thessalonians 2:2, Paul calls him 'The man of sin' and 'Son of perdition.' John calls him 'Antichrist' and 'The beast.'

The dictator is best known as the coming Antichrist, for he is the second person of the evil trinity. He is given several things. First, Satan gives him a throne. This simply means he will have much of the devil in him and he will occupy a place of great prominence in the world system. Then he is given 'a mouth speaking great things and blasphemies.' This man will ridicule God and all who believe in Him. People do that today, believing in atheism, evolution and other ridiculous things, but this will be nothing compared with the Antichrist's blasphemies. Thirdly, he will be given great authority. Obviously as world ruler he will have that position. He will control the world's political affairs. He will have full power over all the world's finance and food supplies, travel and so on. He will rule supreme. Friend, *the Antichrist is coming and probably is here already*, waiting on the sidelines to take over Europe, and then later to rule the world. 'Great authority', yes, he certainly will be supreme.

John tells us that this dictator or beast will rise out of the sea. This simply means he will be from among the nations – a political leader. Men speculate today about different political leaders, but he definitely will not be revealed until after the Rapture of the saints. The Bible says 'All the world wondered after the beast.' He will be a fascinating figure. People all over will worship the dragon, and they will also worship the dictator or beast. He will appear to be supreme.

The great radio Bible teacher, Dr MR DeHaan, wrote 'Terrible days are ahead. The rumblings of the coming judgment era can be heard ... Inventions like the atomic bomb have made men tremble.' There is only one way to escape this dictator, friend, and that is by repenting and asking the Lord Jesus Christ to save us. The Bible says in several places 'Whosoever shall call on the name of the Lord shall be saved.' Have you made that call? If so, you are safe. If not, then do it now. The Bible says 'Now is the accepted time; behold, now is the day of salvation' (2 Corinthians 6:2).

There is so much we can say about the dictator, but let us look now at the third person of the trinity of evil:-

THE DECEIVER

Revelation 13:11 says 'And I beheld another beast coming up out of the earth.' This beast is the deceiver or the false prophet. He will be the right hand of the dictator. He will carry out his orders and he will see that they are enforced. The Bible says that this beast or deceiver will have 'all the power of the first beast.' He will compel the nations to bow down and worship the dictator. John also says 'He doeth great wonders, so that he maketh fire come down from heaven on the earth in the sight of men.' He will do great miracles, and he will have a great statue of the first beast made and erected and he will enable that statue to speak and cause those that will not worship it to be executed.

People sometimes talk of 'The Mark of the Beast.' Well, Revelation 13:16 describes this. The false prophet, or deceiver will devise a mark to be put on the forehead or right hand of people all over the world. Verse 17 says 'that no man might buy or sell, save he that had the mark.' What the mark will be one cannot tell, but today, by using implants, it is very simple to put a pin-head identifying mark in the forehead or right hand. It would disfigure no one but with the use of an infra red light it would be seen immediately. Identification would be in order and any business could be carried out. Without that mark one will be unable to buy food. Death by starvation will follow, or execution by the beast's agents. Do you wish to be here then, my friend? Escape now, by turning to the Lord Jesus for salvation.

> Redemption! Oh wonderful story –
> Glad message for you and for me;
> That Jesus has purchased our pardon
> And paid all the debt on the tree.

It is so important to be saved and know it. The world is rushing on madly to death and destruction. This beast – the deceiver, or false prophet – will head up the world's religions to give all worship to the Antichrist or first beast. Today in the ecumenical movement we see the way being prepared. New

Agers also are working for a world religion, and that will come in the second half of the Tribulation Period. Today the present pope is making overtures to the leaders of many false and pagan religions to unite with Rome.

We are not told what the mark of the beast will be, but that does not matter. We are told though that the number of his name is 666. However, he will still be a mere man, but one who is empowered by the dragon – Satan himself. As the Holy Spirit directs worship to God the Father and the Lord Jesus, so this evil beast or deceiver will direct worship to the dragon and the dictator or Antichrist. He will use Jerusalem as the centre of a world religious system knowing that the Lord Jesus Christ was there. He will endeavour to make the world believe that the Antichrist is truly the saviour of mankind, but he will be vicious and destroy all who oppose him. People must realise that when he makes the statue of the Antichrist speak, Protestants and Roman Catholics, Jews and Gentiles will all have to bow and worship or be killed. The false prophet is Satan's hit man. He will be the great deceiver. The Bible says 'He deceiveth them that dwell on the earth.' Is there perhaps someone reading this today who has been deceived? The truth is found in the Bible. True peace and safety are found in Christ alone. Will you trust Him?

We have considered briefly The Dragon, The Dictator and The Deceiver. Finally, let us look at:-

THE DEPRIVED

Revelation 13:15 indicates that all who will not receive the mark of the beast and all who will not worship the statue of the Antichrist must be killed. These people are the deprived. They will be deprived of their lives! There certainly will be many decent people alive during the terrifying reign of the Antichrist. Only the born again Christians will be gone. Millions too will have been killed or will be killed by God's coming judgments in the Tribulation Period, and especially the Great Tribulation (the second three and a half years). Many of these people will not accept the mark. Many will out of true sincerity refuse to bow down to a statue. Just the average man, who follows like a sheep, will obey. Today, many political leaders would like to dictate and the European Union is doing that behind our backs. Our laws, based on the Mosaic Law, are being changed without our permission or even knowledge.

Do you, my friend, wish to be here then – to live under the rule of the Antichrist and False Prophet? Do you wish to be faced with the alternative: Receive the mark and worship or die? There will be no concessions, and no considerations, just blind obedience or death.

If you were to be executed, where would you go? The answer is found in Revelation 20:15: 'Whosoever was not found written in the book of life was cast into the lake of fire.' Hell for ever will be your destiny. How can we be sure of that? Well, the Bible makes it clear that all who hear and understand the gospel before the Lord Jesus returns for His Own will have no chance of being saved later. Only today is the day of salvation. People who reject the Lord Jesus now as their Saviour will certainly worship the Antichrist later on.

What is going to happen to the two Beasts? Just listen to John's words in Revelation 19:20: 'These both were cast alive into a lake of fire burning with brimstone.' That will happen when the Lord Jesus Christ returns in power and great glory to take control of the world and rule for a thousand years.

CONCLUSION

You have heard the word. What is your response? Christians have nothing to fear for we shall not be here. Unsaved friend, now is the time to repent. The Lord Jesus came to save you. He loved you so much that He went to the Cross and took your place. Will you not trust Him now as your Saviour?

> The wrath of God that was our due,
> Upon the Lamb was laid;
> And by the shedding of His blood
> The debt for us was paid.

Thank Him now for dying for you! Repent and be saved!

CHAPTER TWELVE
JUDGMENT PREDICTED

Reading: Revelation 14

Text: Revelation 14:19: 'The wrath of God.'

INTRODUCTION

This chapter follows one where the Antichrist and the False Prophet are revealed. They bring endless trouble to the earth, although they establish a form of peace which is controlled by their dictatorship. A dark night usually shows the stars at their brightest, and here, following the terrible darkness of chapter 13, we have a magnificent sunrise in chapter 14. Verses 1 to 5 tell of the Lamb of God standing on Mount Zion with a vast number worshipping him and singing His praise. This chapter presents a series of seven separate visions, none of which is connected. Each is distinct. This chapter is a preview to John of events which he tells us about in chapters 15,16,17, 18 and 19. It is like a table of contents, starting with the beginning of the Tribulation Period and finishing with the close of the seven year period. This overview is interesting. First of all we see:-

ROYALTY

Verse 1 describes the King, the Lord Jesus Christ. John the Baptist, in John 1:29 called Him 'the Lamb of God, Which taketh away the sin of the world.' There are many Scriptures which call the Lord Jesus the Lamb. He was the Lamb, all down the centuries when Israel offered a lamb at the Passover – He was the One for Whom they were supposed to look. As the Lamb of God He went to the Cross of Calvary to make atonement for you and for me. His precious sinless blood was shed to pay the price of our sin. The Bible says 'Without shedding of blood, there is no remission' (Hebrews 9:22). Can I ask, are you saved? Have you been washed in that precious blood? The Lord Jesus Christ, the only begotten and eternal Son of God, left heaven for thirty three years in order to save sinners – men and women, boys and girls. He is the Lamb of God. Is He your Saviour?

He is indeed Royalty, for He belongs to the Royal family of heaven, and here in the first few verses of chapter 14 we see Him being worshipped and praised by the 144,000 Jewish evangelists which God is going to raise up after the Rapture of the Church – people who will proclaim the gospel of the Kingdom. They will proclaim this message during the time when the trinity of evil is controlling things, Satan, the Antichrist and the False Prophet. These Israelis will be saved and transformed after the Rapture, for all who hear and understand the message of salvation will have no chance of being saved later. We live today in the Age of Grace – that period when people may repent of their sin and ask the Lord Jesus to save them and cleanse them with His precious blood.

Here we see the Royal King of kings being worshipped and praised. The 144,000 are singing a great new song. There was much rejoicing as vast numbers of people will be saved in the Tribulation Period, though none of them would have understood the Gospel before. They will not be part of the Church, the Bride of Christ, for that body will be complete when the Rapture takes place.

Christian friend, may I ask: Do you sing the praises of Jesus daily? Is there a song of praise in your heart? He needs and requires our worship and adoration, for He has done so much for us. As the hymn says:-

>Praise the Saviour, ye who know Him;
>Who can tell how much we owe Him?

Gladly let us render to Him
All we are and have.

Let us move on a little in the chapter. It has introduced us to Royalty, but, secondly, we have:-

WRATH

Verses 6 and 7 introduce something different. Here we find one of God's special angels flying throughout the whole earth proclaiming a message of judgment, namely the wrath of God. His message is this: 'Fear God, and give glory to Him; for the hour of His judgment is come.' This message concerning wrath will go forth to give people all over the world an opportunity to repent and worship the Lord. The antichrist will then be ruling.

In a sense, this will be God's last call to a wicked and apostate world. Men and women, boys and girls have to be told again and again that the Lord alone is supreme. He is the Creator and Sustainer of this world of ours, and He needs to be worshipped. When this all happens, the Antichrist and False Prophet will be endeavouring to secure total world supremacy. Through the mark of the beast referred to in chapter 13, no one will be able to buy food or sell things without this mark, and today that mark is being discussed as a means of identification. A tiny implant in the forehead or right hand, almost invisible to the eye, can contain all of one's important details. Through modern science and computers, this is not only possible, but being strongly recommended. Through such means a watch could be kept on suspected terrorists and others.

The message is clear. All who go along with the coming Antichrist will face the terrors of God's wrath. And, in this Gospel Age, people who reject the Lord Jesus Christ as Saviour will also experience this wrath. In Matthew 3:7 the Lord Jesus was speaking to the religious leaders and He said 'Who hath warned you to flee from the wrath to come?' Wrath. The wrath of God is to be feared. In John 3:36 we read these words 'He that believeth on the Son hath everlasting life: and he that believeth not the Son shall not see life; but the wrath of God abideth on him.' Without Christ as one's personal Saviour, we face the wrath of God, for we are simply rejecting His offer of salvation. Romans 1:18 says 'the wrath of God is revealed from heaven against all ungodliness and unrighteousness.' Colossians 3:6 states 'The wrath of God cometh on the children of disobedience.' Today there is no need for anyone to face the wrath of God, for 1 Thessalonians 5:9 tells us 'For God hath not appointed us to wrath, but to obtain salvation by our Lord Jesus Christ.' The choice today is simple and clear. If we repent of all our sin and ask the Lord Jesus Christ to save us and wash us in His precious blood, we are saved – saved eternally. However, if we choose to go our own way, we shall inevitably experience the fiercesome wrath of God, and spend eternity in hell. Unsaved friend, I urge you now to 'Flee from the wrath to come.' God loves people so much that He sent His only begotten Son into the world to save us – to pay the penalty for us. And He did this on the Cross of Calvary. What, my friend, is your response to such love?

As we move on a little farther in Revelation 14 we find:-

RUIN

Yes, ruin is foretold. Verse 7 states 'Babylon is fallen, is fallen.' This is John's introduction to what is described in greater detail in chapter 17. The Babylon of ecumenical Romanism is centred in Rome or the Vatican. We live in a day when many churches and meetings are drawing together to form an eventual world church which the False Prophet initially will use to introduce the worship of the Antichrist. Dr Lehman Strauss stated in one of his books 'Here is a religious system in its most corrupt form. Multitudes are won to it and intoxicated by it.' Roman Catholicism encourages the worship of idols and images of Mary and the saints who are all dead. Jeremiah 50:38 describes Babylon (or Rome) as 'the land of graven images, and they are mad upon their idols.'

All who worship pagan idols will face eternal ruin. And all who worship the image of the beast in the Tribulation Period will also face ruin. What does the Bible say? Listen to verses 9 to 11: 'The third angel followed them, saying with a loud voice, If any man worship the beast and his image, and receive his mark in his forehead, or in his hand, the same shall drink of the wine of the wrath of God, which is poured out without mixture into the cup of His indignation; and he shall be tormented with fire and brimstone in the presence of the holy angels, and in the presence of the Lamb: And the smoke of their torment ascendeth up for ever and ever: and they shall have no rest day nor night, who worship the beast and his image, and whosoever receiveth the mark of his name.' What a prospect! And everyone who is not saved will probably receive the Antichrist's mark. Today is your opportunity to be saved.

Dr Lee Roberson, in one of his books, tells the story of Rose Crawford. She was 80 years of age and had been blind for 50 years. With modern technology she underwent surgery. When the Canadian doctor removed her bandages, she cried out 'I just can't believe it!' Fifty years in darkness were now transformed. The world she saw was dazzling and beautiful. And so it is today when people trust the Saviour. The man whom Jesus healed called out 'Once I was blind, but now I can see' (John 9:25). Are *you*, friend, still in darkness? The poet penned these lines:-

> Ye dwellers in darkness, with sin-blinded eyes,
> The Light of the world is Jesus!
> Go, wash at His bidding, and light will arise,
> The Light of the world is Jesus!
> Come to the Light, 'tis shining for thee;
> Sweetly the light has dawned upon me;
> Once I was blind, but now I can see;
> The Light of the world is Jesus!

We have seen that Revelation 14 speaks of Royalty, Wrath and Ruin. Finally, we are faced with:-

RETRIBUTION

The last seven verses of this chapter spell out retribution. This is a fore view of Armageddon and the very end. The Lord Jesus Christ has a sharp sickle in His hand. He is going to reap. He is going to deal with the earth for its endless wickedness. He is about to pronounce judgment and show His final retribution on men and women who have rejected Him. The harvest of sin is ripe and the Lord is about to cut it down. These few verses are a preview of Revelation 17, 18 and 19. Verse 18 tells how God's mighty angel cried out 'Thrust in thy sharp sickle.' The following verse tells us that these clusters are to be gathered and cast 'into the great winepress of the wrath of God.' This is the picture of the final stages of the Great Tribulation. The various tribulation judgments will have passed. Hundreds of millions of people will have perished. Now, it is the battle of Armageddon, and the world's armies will be there in Israel to finally destroy God's earthly people and wipe them out, but lo and behold the Lord Jesus Christ suddenly appears in the heavens riding a great white horse, and leading the armies of heaven. This is made clear in chapter 19. The Antichrist and the False Prophet will be taken and dealt with. Chapter 19 tells of their eternal destiny: 'And the beast was taken, and with him the false prophet that wrought miracles before him, with which he deceived them that had received the mark of the beast, and them that worshipped his image. These both were cast alive into a lake burning with fire and brimstone.' The millions of soldiers who were there in that scene in Israel will be wiped out. Back in Revelation 14, verse 20 tells of God's retribution against this world army. 'Blood came out of the winepress, even unto the horses bridles, by the space of a thousand and six hundred furlongs' (that is, two hundred miles, which is the length of Israel today from North to South).

JUDGMENT PREDICTED

Judgment is fast coming. The whole world will see Who is finally in control. Man will have had his day, and the Lord Jesus Christ will be taking control. The Bible tells us that He will reign from Jerusalem for a thousand years and then this earth will know what peace really is. Men and women all over will have to bow to Him. As Paul says in Philippians 2:10 'Every knee shall bow . . . and every tongue confess that Jesus Christ is Lord to the glory of God the Father.'

Every human being today is in danger. The Bible states quite clearly 'After death, judgment.' Many will be all right, for the Lord Jesus Christ lovingly bore the judgment for us. He paid the price for our sin two thousand years ago. The Bible says 'God is not willing that any should perish, but that all should come to repentance' (2 Peter 3:9). There we have the secret. True repentance is a *must*. We have to be sorry for our sin and tell the Lord that. Then, and only then, can we find the Saviour. The Bible says 'Believe on the Lord Jesus Christ, and thou shalt be saved' (Acts 16:31). Today you have your own personal opportunity to repent and trust the Saviour. Remember, tomorrow could be too late, for the Lord Jesus Christ may return at any moment and remove from this world all who are His.

CONCLUSION

Revelation 14 is very solemn in its closing verses. The opening verses portray the Lamb of God being praised, worshipped and adored. Do you know Him? Would you not like to get to know this wonderful Saviour? He has saved many of us, and He is waiting and ready to save anyone who will repent and trust Him. Will you do that *now*? If not, our text must burn into your mind and stay there: 'the wrath of God.' It is real and it is permanent. 'The wrath of God.'

> Sinner, heed the warning voice,
> Make the Lord your final choice,
> Then all heaven will rejoice:

Be in time!
Come from darkness into light,
Come, let Jesus make you right;
Come, and start for heaven tonight;
Be in time!

CHAPTER THIRTEEN

THE SEVEN VIAL JUDGMENTS

Reading: Revelation 15 and 16:1-12 and 17-21

Text: Revelation 15:1: 'The seven last plagues; in them is filled up the wrath of God.'

INTRODUCTION

In Revelation chapters 15 and 16, the apostle John is given a preview of things to come. There are two groups of people described here: the unbelievers who face the wrath of a holy God, and His own blood-washed people who rejoice in their Saviour and His salvation. To which of these groups do YOU belong? Every one of us is either saved or lost. There is no in-between position. The Bible says to anyone in doubt 'If thou shalt confess with thy mouth the Lord Jesus, and believe in thine heart that God hath raised Him from the dead, thou shalt be saved' (Romans 10:9). The Bible also proclaims that 'Whosoever shall call upon the name of the Lord shall be saved' (Romans 10:13). If anyone reading this is in doubt, then make your call now, for today is the day of salvation. Tomorrow could be too late, for the Lord Jesus is coming again and will remove all who are saved from this earth to be with Him for ever.

These two chapters break up simply into three sections. First, we have The Triumph. Next, we see The Temple, and finally we have The Torture. Let us look, first of all at:-

THE TRIUMPH

These two chapters deal with the second half of the Tribulation Period. And at its close John sees a great company of redeemed souls, singing and rejoicing in heaven. These were people who had been saved in the Tribulation Period and in most cases, if not all, had been martyred. The Bible says they 'had gotten the victory over the beast, and over his image, and over his mark, and over the number of his name.'

These men and women were martyrs for the Lord Jesus, and here John sees them singing 'the song of Moses, the servant of God, and the song of the Lamb.' What was 'the song of Moses'? We find this recorded in Exodus 15:1-19. Verses 1, 3 and 18 give due praise to the Lord for His all-victorious doings. He conquered Pharaoh long ago, and now He has conquered the Antichrist. In reality, this has not yet taken place, but it will happen seven years after the Lord Jesus Christ takes away His people at the Rapture. Jesus is coming soon! Are you ready? Are you saved?

Triumph. Yes, indeed. These Tribulation saints will sing of God's deliverance and the downfall of His enemies. The 'song of the Lamb' is simply a song of praise to the One Who has saved them. Here, we must point out that no one who hears and understands the Gospel today will have a chance of being saved in the Tribulation. These people died for their faith in the Lord Jesus and refused the mark of the beast and would not worship Satan's evil man, but now in Glory, they sing in triumph.

The second scene is that of:-

THE TEMPLE

Our text states 'The seven last plagues – in them is filled up the wrath of God.' Revelation 15:5 mentions 'The temple of the testimony.' This refers to the Holy of Holies where the ark of the testimony was kept. Dr Lehman Strauss explains this in these words. 'The ark speaks of the faithfulness of God in keeping His covenants. Under the Law of Moses the holiest of all was concealed from the eyes of the people. Mystery shrouded that sacred area. But, here the mystery of God is finished. The way into the holiest is now open to all the redeemed, including the tribulation saints.' We who know the Lord today have complete access into the presence of the Lord. The Temple. This is where the Lord dwells and this is where we can come with our burdens, our troubles and our joys. As the hymn says, 'Take it to the Lord in prayer.'

The Temple in heaven is the place where the Lord is worshipped, and it is here that He makes His judgments. It is from here that the bad news for mankind is going to proceed. The Bible says in Revelation 15:6, 'The seven angels came out of the temple, having the seven plagues.' These seven angels have been deputed by God to vindicate His holiness and execute His wrath on a Christ-rejecting world. Under the Antichrist, during the Tribulation Period, things will have reached such a pitch of evil that the Lord is going to have these seven vials of His wrath emptied upon the earth. Do you, friend, anticipate being there? If not, make sure you are saved and washed in the precious blood. As the hymn writer once put it:-

On yonder hill of Calvary,

The sinner's only hope and plea,

Christ gave Himself for such as we –

On Calvary, dark Calvary.

'The seven last plagues; in them is filled up the wrath of God.' What words! We have seen The Triumph and also The Temple. Let us look now at:-

THE TORTURE

Under the reign of the coming Antichrist, the world will have become unbelievably evil. It is bad enough today, but when all the Christians are gone, terrible corruption will set in. Here in these two chapters John is receiving a preview of the torture which will arrive on the earth during the latter half of the Tribulation. The Bible does say 'God is love' (1 John 4:8), but He is also a God of justice, and man's rebellion will be sorely punished. Seven vials of

God's wrath are to be poured out on a Christ-rejecting world. In Psalm 75:8 the Bible says 'In the hand of the Lord there is a cup.' And also in Psalm 116:13 it states 'I will take the cup of salvation, and call upon the name of the Lord.' Today is still 'escape' time. Anyone can repent now and escape the coming judgments. Remember, our text says 'The seven last plagues; in them is filled up the wrath of God.' Yes, the *wrath of God*. It is bad enough to face the wrath of an angry person, but the anger of God . . . that is totally different.

Torture. Yes, God is going to send seven different plagues on the earth during the last three and a half years of the Tribulation. It is not a pleasant prospect, and some people may be horrified, but the good part is that there will be none of the saved people alive today here on earth to face the torture which is coming. Revelation 3:10 gives today's Christian this promise: 'I will keep thee from the hour of temptation (tribulation) which shall come upon the whole world.' So we who are God's dear people have nothing to fear. He has saved us through the shed blood of His dear Son, and we shall be safe in the glory land when this torture falls on the earth.

The Lord's our Rock, in Him we hide;

A shelter in the time of storm!

Secure whatever ill betide:

A shelter in the time of storm!

Are you, dear friend, safe and secure? If not, repent now and ask the Lord to save you.

The torture is going to be in seven parts. There are seven different judgments which the Lord is going to send before the final battle, Armageddon. We shall look at these one by one. First, we have:-

THE PLAGUE OF SORES

Chapter 16:1 states 'There fell a noisome and grievous sore upon the men which had the mark of the beast, and upon them which worshipped his image.' This judgment is on people only, no animal will suffer, and it will be specially for all who worship the Antichrist and have his mark. This judgment of sores would appear to be some sort of nasty boils, and these usually come about because of bad blood. People who are saved have been cleansed by the precious blood of the Lord Jesus, and there will be many saved during the Tribulation under the preaching of the 144,000 Jewish evangelists – people who never previously heard or understood the way of salvation. This plague reminds us of the plague of boils which the Lord sent on Pharaoh and the Egyptians when they would not allow Israel to go to the Promised Land. This is a punishment for idolatry and apostasy. It will affect all who worship the beast. In the Lord Jesus, people can be healed today – cured of their sin problem. The Lord is able to do this now for anyone who will repent and trust Him as their personal Saviour:-

> Have you been to Jesus for the cleansing power?
> Are you washed in the blood of the Lamb?
> Are you fully trusting in His grace this hour?
> Are you washed in the blood of the Lamb?

THE PLAGUE OF BLOOD

The next judgment is mentioned in verse 3. 'The second angel poured out his vial upon the sea; and it became as the blood of a dead man: and every living soul died in the sea.' This sort of thing happened in a minor way when the waters of Egypt turned to blood in Pharaoh's day. This torture simply indicated that all the fish will die – fishing and shipping industries will cease. The smell will be terrible – a rotten smell, like that of dead bodies. That is what God's Word says. It will be a foul smell of corruption, and all over the world people will find it impossible to escape this. Just imagine trying to escape from the stench of rotten blood. This will indeed be a severe judgment.

The third vial of God's wrath is:-

FRESH WATER TURNED TO BLOOD

In the second judgment the sea turned to blood, but verse 4 tells us 'The third angel poured out his vial upon the rivers and fountains of waters; and they became blood.' This angel goes on to say that the Antichrist and his followers had taken the life blood of vast numbers, and now God was giving these people blood to drink. The rivers and lakes and all the springs will become blood. What a prospect! What does our text say about these plagues? 'In them is filled up the wrath of God.' Men and women will keep on rejecting the Lord, for they will continue to be deceived by the Antichrist and False Prophet.

The Bible says to us today to repent and turn from sin and trust the Lord Jesus Christ. 'Today, if ye will hear His voice, harden not your hearts' (Psalm 95:6-7). Will you, my unsaved friend, repent now and trust the Saviour? He is waiting and willing to save you.

We find the next vial judgment in verses 8 and 9:-

THE PLAGUE OF THE SCORCHING SUN

'The fourth angel poured out his vial upon the sun; and power was given unto him to scorch men with fire. And men were scorched with great heat, and blasphemed the name of God, which hath power over these plagues: and they repented not to give Him glory.' People all over will know that these plagues will be from the Lord, but they will still not repent of their sin and wickedness. There is a lot of preaching today which omits repentance, but that word is vital for salvation. A 'come to Jesus' message is not true salvation. The Bible teaches us that we have to repent and then trust the Saviour. In Luke 21:25 the Lord Jesus foretold something of this. He said, 'There shall be signs in the sun, and in the moon, and in the stars; and upon the earth distress of nations.' Scientists today tell us that if the tilt of the earth by two degrees were to take place, the world would be scorched in places. Heat waves will be nothing in comparison with this terrifying judgment.

Torture, sure. It is coming during the Great Tribulation, shortly before the battle of Armageddon.

What about the next Torture? Verses 10 and 11 introduce us to:-

THE PLAGUE OF DARKNESS

The Bible says 'The fifth angel poured out his vial upon the seat of the beast; and his kingdom was full of darkness; and they gnawed their tongues for pain. And they blasphemed the God of heaven because of their pains and their sores, and repented not of their deeds.' There will still be no repentance. Man as a whole will be so controlled by sin and the Antichrist that there will be no change. Men and women will see for themselves that their god – the beast – has no power to prevent the judgments of Almighty God. This darkness will centre over the place where the Antichrist will have his headquarters and all around that area. We are not told that this judgment will be worldwide. However, it will have a worldwide effect. The book of Joel mentions this in chapter 2:2: 'A day of darkness and of gloominess, a day of clouds and of thick darkness.' Our text says 'The seven last plagues; in them is filled up the wrath of God.'

Number six is introduced in verse 12:-

THE PLAGUE OF THE VAST ARMY

The River Euphrates is to be dried up to enable the vast army from the East – 200 million men – to come West with ease. Armageddon is now at hand, for that army is bound for Israel.

THE FINAL PLAGUE

Verse 15 announces 'Behold I come as a thief.' Here we have the announcement that the Lord Jesus Christ, Himself, is coming to this earth to conquer at Armageddon, destroy the Antichrist and False Prophet in the Lake of Fire, and set up His world government. His coming will be like that of a thief – sudden, and without announcement. The wicked all over the world will have to bow to Him and obey His rule.

This coming reminds us that Jesus is coming back any day to remove all who are saved. Are you ready? Are you saved? If not, you will face the torture that is coming on the earth, and eventually you will be condemned to hell, for ever and ever. The Bible says 'Believe on the Lord Jesus Christ, and thou shalt be saved' (Acts 16:31). It also says 'Whosoever shall call on the name of the Lord shall be saved' (Romans 10:13).

> Jesus is waiting, oh come to Him now –
> Waiting today, waiting today!
> Come with thy sins, at His feet lowly bow;
> Come, and no longer delay.

CHAPTER FOURTEEN

THE DOOM OF THE VATICAN

Reading: Revelation 17

Text: Revelation 17:1b: 'I will shew unto thee the judgment of the great whore that sitteth upon many waters.'

INTRODUCTION

The Doom of the Vatican is our subject, and we find it recorded in Revelation 17. Many people today accept the Church of Rome as 'Christian', but it is not. It is an apostate church – Satan's counterfeit – and God is determined to destroy it in the not too distant future. Rome, or the Vatican, is probably the world's greatest religious and political force. Its history tells of intrigue, hatred and murder. Wherever Rome is in a substantial majority, Christians are persecuted and, in many cases, killed. The Church of Rome seeks world supremacy. Many wars have been fought because of the intrigues and ambitions of Rome – wars such as World Wars 1 and 2, and the Vietnam war also. Today Rome is showing friendship to many religions in an effort to have a one-world religion dominated by the Vatican. Through New Age teaching in schools and colleges a major effort is being made to establish a one-world religion and a one-world government. The Bible calls the Vatican 'Mystery, Babylon the Great, the mother of harlots and abominations of the earth.' These are God's words, not mine! 'Mother of harlots.' The Bible gives us a detailed description of this evil church and we shall consider this now. Let us look at:-

ITS DETAILED DESCRIPTION

Revelation 17 gives a detailed description of this wicked system. Rome traces its history back to Babylon and all the pagan rites carried out there. Babylon is mentioned in Genesis where the people rebelled against the Lord and sought to build their own way to heaven via the tower of Babel. They worshipped their king, Nimrod, and he got them to worship his wife Semiramis and their baby son Tammuz. Babylonianism was basically an anti-God movement. In it one learned to confess to the priest of Babylon. The priest then had that person in his power. The Babylonian high priest was called The Pontiff. Many centuries passed and eventually the Pontiff was the reigning king of Pergamos in Turkey. When he died in the year 133 BC, he passed on the Headship of the Babylonian priesthood to Rome. When the Etruscans went to Italy from Pergamos, they took with them the Babylonian religion and rites, and set up a new Pontiff or Poe as their ruler. Julius Caesar became Pontiff in 74 BC, and eleven years later he was made Supreme Pontiff of the Babylonian Order. Rome then became the centre of the Babylonian religion, with confession and the worship of woman and child. Many Christians do not know this, and many good Protestants are unaware where Roman Catholicism originated. In 376 AD, the Roman Emperor Gratian refused the title of Pontiff, apparently for Christian principles, and the title passed to the Bishop of Rome where it has stayed ever since.

Rome is described in God's Word as 'Babylon the great, the mother of harlots and abominations of the earth.' She is also spoken of as 'the great whore.' Revelation 17 tells how Romanism has flirted with kings and political leaders all over the world. Verse 3 tells how this 'great whore' rides upon a beast which has seven heads and ten horns, and we know from other portions of Scripture that this refers to the kingdom of the Antichrist which we see

THE DOOM OF THE VATICAN

forming today in the European Union. Verse 4 describes the woman as 'arrayed in purple and scarlet' – the colours of the Vatican. This detailed description does not present us with a picture of a holy church proclaiming God's way of salvation! No, this is a corrupt, immoral and pagan church. Salvation is through the Lord Jesus Christ alone and trough faith in His precious shed blood! Can I ask you today if you are saved? Have you been redeemed, 'not with corruptible things such as silver and gold, but with the precious blood of Christ' (1 Peter 1:19)?

Continuing with the detailed description, we find in verse 6 that Mystery Babylon or Rome is 'drunken with the blood of the saints, and with the blood of the martyrs of Jesus.' Down through the centuries Roman Catholicism has caused the death of millions upon millions of true believers. Just to mention a few, we think of the Huegenots in France, the Scottish Covenanters, and great men of God like Bishops Ridley and Latimer. Today Rome still kills true Christians in places like Columbia and Yugoslavia, where the Croats murdered nearly a million Serbs during the last war because they would not turn and become Roman Catholics. Yes, the great whore is truly 'drunken with the blood of the saints.'

Now, let us look secondly at:-

ITS DEVILISH DECEPTION

Rome is called 'the mother of harlots.' Why? Well there are obviously many smaller harlots! Younger ones! Since the Reformation we have many other churches – Presbyterian, Anglican, Methodist, Baptist, Pentecostal also Brethren assemblies and so on. Today, there is a major effort being made to establish a world church. This is being done through the ecumenical movement and also to a much greater extent through the charismatic movement. The common denominator is not salvation, which the Bible states is through Christ alone and by faith alone. No! It is excitement, experiences and a getting together of all kinds under the charismatic banner. Doctrine does not seem to matter any more. The Word of God commands true believers to come out from such churches and meetings and be separate. 2 Corinthians 6:17 says 'Come out from among them and be ye separate, saith the Lord, and touch not the unclean thing.' The name 'Babylon' means 'confusion', and surely many people today are confused. Christians, our lives must be *Bible-centred.* Can we have anything to do with a false religion whose churches and cathedrals are filled with idols and images? The Bible thoroughly condemns such things. In Exodus 20:4 and 5, God says 'Thou shalt not make unto thee any graven image . . . Thou shalt not bow down thyself to them, nor serve them.'

This devilish deception of creating a world church is from the pit. When men and women are saved, we are one. We belong to the one true church, the Bride of Christ. Can I ask again, are you saved? Do you belong to the Lord? Are you His? If not, then you must repent of your sin and trust the Saviour today! The Bible says today is the day of salvation, not tomorrow. 'Now is the accepted time, behold, now is the day of salvation' (2 Corinthians 6:2). Do not be deceived by anyone saying you need to join a church or be baptised. You need to be saved! The Bible says again and again 'Whosoever shall call on the name of the Lord shall be saved.'

The world church and the charismatic movement will lead to hell – to a lost eternity. Put your trust in the Saviour NOW, while you may. Do not be deceived!

> Come and He will give you rest;
> Trust Him, for His Word is plain;
> He will save the sinfulest;
> Christ receiveth sinful men.

ITS DETERMINED DOMINATION

Revelation 17:18 says 'The woman which thou sawest is that great city, which reigneth over the kings of the earth.' There is no other city in the world which has dominated kings and rulers – just Rome! Rome's influence is

THE DOOM OF THE VATICAN

felt and seen worldwide. The Vatican is determined to dominate and control the whole world. Our text reminds us that the great whore 'sitteth upon many waters.' Verse 15 explains 'The waters which thou sawest, where the whore sitteth, are peoples, and multitudes, and nations, and tongues.' This woman, Rome, is determined to dominate the whole earth! The great apostle Peter warned us to beware. In 2 Peter 1:1 and 2 he says 'There shall be false teachers among you, who privily shall bring in damnable heresies . . . and many shall follow their pernicious ways.' That is why we see charismatics who are confused mixing with Roman Catholic priests.

There is a day coming when the dictator of Europe – the Antichrist, whom we read about in various Scriptures – will use this apostate world church, the Great Whore, for his own ends. The world church – Romanism plus all the others who join in – will help direct worship eventually to the Antichrist. True believers will be away, for the Lord Jesus Christ is coming again and He will take all who are His home to glory!

Many efforts are being made today to establish world peace, and while that may in itself be a good objective, it never will be until the Prince of Peace comes to reign. The world will accept the rule of the Antichrist and also the False Prophet, and they will use the Scarlet Woman – this world church we are talking about – for their own ends. Revelation 13 tells us that the world will wonder after the Beast or Antichrist. The day will come when people all over the world will be commanded to worship the Antichrist. Those who refuse to do this will die, and all who refuse to have his mark on their forehead or in their right hand will be executed. Christian, thank the Lord that we shall not be here! Unbeliever, trust the Lord Jesus now before it is too late!

World dominion for Mystery Babylon the Great is coming. Remember, the European Union is based on the Treaty of Rome! We have looked at the Great Whore – its Detailed Description, its Devilish Deception and its Determined Domination. Finally, we must consider:-

ITS DEVASTATING DOOM

Yes, friend, Rome is doomed! Our text says 'I will shew thee the *judgment* of the great whore that sitteth upon many waters.' The church of Rome is deceiving many people today. We are not against any Roman Catholic person, but against a system which God is determined to destroy. Roman Catholics need the Saviour, and we need to tell them that He is the only way to heaven. The Lord Jesus said 'I am the way, the truth and the life; no man cometh unto the Father but by Me' (John 14:6). Mary cannot help. The saints cannot either. No priest can save a lost soul. All the confessions in the world cannot help. All the penances are no good. We just simply have to come as sinners to the One Who died in our place at Calvary. Christ alone can save! And He will save YOU today if you ask Him.

Its Devastating Doom is foretold in Revelation 17. When the Antichrist is being worshipped himself, he will no longer need a super-church. The various rulers of the European Union under him will turn against this mystery Babylon, the great whore, and will destroy her. Verses 16 and 17 tell us what is going to happen. 'The ten horns which thou sawest upon the beast, these shall hate the whore, and shall make her desolate and naked, and shall eat her flesh, and burn her with fire. For God hath put in their hearts to fulfil His will.' The ten nations – the Bible says ten, so there will be changes coming – will hate the world church, not needing religion any more for their own ends. The whore will be destroyed. Her wealth and her possessions will be taken and used. All who worship in that church will find that they will have to worship Satan's man, the Antichrist, or be executed.

Our text reminds us that God has said 'I will show thee the judgment of the great whore that sitteth upon many waters.' Its devastating destruction is ahead. The Vatican is doomed. Rome depends on power – power supplied through governments which Rome controls and influences. When the ten-kingdom federation turns against Mystery Babylon the Great, she is finished. That day is approaching.

THE DOOM OF THE VATICAN 123

Today the woman rides the beast. The European Union is already under the control of Rome. The Treaty of Rome is perhaps the greatest Common Market document and it shows who is leader. Britain should never have been joined in with Europe, for the Lord put the sea between us to keep us separate. Dr DeHaan, the great Bible teacher and radio broadcaster, wrote some years ago 'The last few years have seen an alarming increase in the limitations imposed upon the free expression of our religious views and the liberties of teaching the full counsel of God. Powerful agencies are at work day and night to stop the preaching of the fundamental Gospel, and godless men who know neither Christ nor spiritual truth are posing as authorities to tell us what we can and what we cannot preach.' How much longer we have is uncertain. One thing for sure is that the Lord Jesus Christ is coming again! Are you ready? Are you saved? If not, you can repent now and ask the Lord to save you.

Today the woman rides the beast. Rome is hoping to control the whole world, but she never will. Satan's man, the Antichrist, will, but only for a short while. During his reign people will be unable to buy or sell unless they have his mark on their foreheads or on their right hand. People today are being conditioned for this through having their own bank numbers, plastic card money and an eventual cashless society. See how many firms like one to pay by Direct Debit! This gives them power over people's bank accounts.

'I will shew thee the judgment of the great whore that sitteth upon many waters.' Yes, judgment is coming. Clarence Larkin, the great prophetic Bible teacher, states that the Antichrist, when he is established, 'will not permit any worship that does not centre in himself.' Roman Catholicism and the ecumenical church will be destroyed – utterly!

Rome's influence today is worldwide, and it appears to be increasing. But Rome is doomed, and also every soul who does not know the Saviour is doomed. The Bible says in John 3:18 'He that believeth not is condemned already.' Let me remind you that 'God so loved the world that He gave His only begotten Son, that whosoever believeth in Him should not perish but have everlasting life' (John 3:16). Will you, my unsaved friend, believe now? A Christian is not a religious person, but one who has repented and trusted Christ; one who is 'in Christ.'

Rome claims to be the one true church, but she is not, and she is doomed for destruction. Rome preaches another gospel and teaches another way of salvation. The Lord Jesus made it clear that He alone is the way of salvation. He said in John 14:6, 'I am the way, the truth and the life; no man cometh unto the Father *but by Me.*' In Acts 4:12 the Bible states, 'Neither is there salvation *in any other:* for there is none other name under heaven given among men whereby we must be saved.' The worship of Mary is wrong, for she spoke in Luke 1:47 of the Lord being her Saviour. The Bible says in 1 Timothy 2:5-6, 'There is one God and one Mediator between God and men, the man Christ Jesus; Who gave Himself a ransom for all.' He alone can go before a holy God and tell Him that He paid the price for us. Do you believe this? The Vatican is doomed. Are YOU?

CONCLUSION

Our text says 'I will shew thee the judgment of the great whore that sitteth upon many waters.' As we close, may I remind you that judgment is ahead for all who are not saved. 'After this the judgment.' My unsaved friend, I plead with you to repent NOW and ask the Lord Jesus Christ to save you and cleanse you with His precious blood. Then and only then, will you be saved. Religion cannot save, only Christ. Will you trust Him NOW?

> Come to the Saviour, make no delay;
> Here in His Word He has shown us the way;
> Here in our midst He's standing today,
> Tenderly saying, Come.

Will YOU come?

CHAPTER FIFTEEN
POLITICAL BABYLON

Reading: Revelation 18

INTRODUCTION

In the Book of Revelation two different Babylons are mentioned. To many a reader they might appear to be one and the same, but as we look closer and carefully examine the Word of God, we see that they are distinctly separate. In Revelation 17 we have *ecclesiastical* Babylon, while in chapter 18 we read of *political* Babylon.

The name 'Babylon' makes one think of the ancient and historic city which was the head of a great world empire thousands of years ago. Originally, it came into being in the days after the Flood, when God had purged the earth of its extreme wickedness. It is amazing how this wonderful Book – the Bible – has not only the message of salvation. It records for us the main historical events which were to shape the world's history as well. And so, we have recorded for us in Genesis 10 and 11 how the city of Babylon came into being.

Not long after the Flood, the descendants of Noah forgot the lesson which they should have learned, and turned their backs on God. They moved into a land which became known as Shinar. Their leader was a man called Nimrod, and he instigated the building of a great city which became one of the wonders of the world. In the centre of the city was a great temple for the worship of Belus, the Babylonian god, who was later called Baal. Babylon was a great city, fourteen miles square, with a deep moat filled with water as a protection against invasion. The walls were 80 feet thick and 200 feet high. Nimrod also built a great tower – the Tower of Babel. This tower had a base of stone 300 feet square and 110 feet high. The second stage of this tower was 260 feet square and 60 feet high. The third, fourth, fifth and sixth stages were each slightly smaller, and at the top of the sixth stage – 300 feet up – was the sanctuary of Belus.

The purpose of Nimrod and his Babylonian confederates was to create a world power – both religious and political. In the Tower we see the religious side, and in the city we have the political side. In Genesis 11:4 we read 'And they said, Go to, let us build us a city and a tower, whose top may reach unto heaven; and let us make us a name, lest we be scattered abroad upon the face of the whole earth.' These people wanted power and security, just as we see it today in the 21st century. Of course, God had provided security – in the shed blood. In Genesis 3:21 He had made plain His way 'Unto Adam also and to his wife did the Lord God make coats of skins, and clothed them.' These were but a foreshadowing of what Christ was to accomplish for the believer. But the Babylonians denied this. Their aim was to reach God and heaven by *works* – the work of their hands. As one well-known writer has put it, 'The dream of man, separated from God, is a man-made way of salvation by works, a universal federation of nations under one dictatorial leader, a universal church which denies the blood, a universal language dominated by a super-state which will formulate the policies of both government and religion.' That, my friend, is the position today! In ancient Babylon and its Tower we have a picture of the last days. In Revelation 17 we read of Ecclesiastical Babylon and its doom, while in chapter 18 we have political Babylon and its doom.

First of all, let us consider:-

ITS DESIRE

We see that in political Babylon there is to be one great desire and aim: World Unity! The days in which we live, with the constant threat of thermo-nuclear warfare, the up-rising of minority peoples, and world conditions in general, all point to the need for a united and powerful world government. In political Babylon there will be that, but only for a very short time. This desire for unity is already present and quite manifest. In fact, it has almost become an obsession with many people.

After the True Church has been caught away at the Rapture, political Babylon will come into being. The nations will unite for peace and safety in an organisation far more powerful than the United Nations organisation. The world does not know Christ and has no time for Him, and yet He is our only hope. Men today are bent on unity. Wherever we turn, the story is the same. Business concerns unite to form strong companies. Nations unite with others for strength. Church leaders are talking incessantly of unity, even with Rome. Forgotten is the story of the martyred saints. Forgotten is the blood that was shed by our forefathers that we might have freedom of worship. Forgotten are the days when men had to read the Bible in secret. The one great desire today is for unity. Humanly speaking, one cannot condemn the universal desire for peace and unity, and when men leave God out of the picture then it is natural for them to fall back on erring, human reasoning which falls far short of the required standards. Dr E Schuyler English has rightly said 'Evil men and seducers wax worse and worse. There is much talk of ecclesiastical union. A day will come, as some desire already, when Protestantism will join hands with the Roman Catholic Church in the name of tolerance and religious power. Protestantism as a whole is swiftly drifting towards shipwreck. Modern Paines, Voltaires, Rousseaus and Ingersolls teach infidelity and godlessness openly in schools and colleges, denying the supernatural – God and His Christ – and deifying man. The time has already come when men will no longer endure sound doctrine but, having itching ears, gather to themselves, after their own desires, teachers who turn away from the truth and to fables (2 Timothy 4:3,4). Apostasy is fast enveloping Christendom.'

This, then, is political Babylon's great desire.

ITS DICTATOR

Secondly, we must think of its Dictator. Political Babylon will be ruled by a Dictator who is described for us in various parts of the Bible. In Revelation 13 in particular, we learn of this person who is yet to come forward – see verse 1: 'And I stood upon the sand of the sea, and saw a beast rise up out of the sea, having seven heads and ten horns, and upon his horns ten crowns, and upon his heads the name of blasphemy.' We read of him also in Daniel chapter 7. Here we are told that he is to rule over a ten-kingdom federation of nations covering the area of the old Roman Empire. Therefore, it will be a European federation of nations which he will lead. Perhaps, already today we see signs of this in the European Common Market.

The Dictator will be given tremendous power, and the whole world will listen to his voice. In Revelation 13:3-4, we read that 'all the world wondered after the beast. And they worshipped the dragon which gave power unto the beast: and they worshipped the beast, saying, Who is like unto the beast? Who is able to make war with him?' This man, the world's last great dictator, will not be revealed until the Rapture of the Church has taken place. In 2 Thessalonians 2 the Apostle Paul makes this clear. Here, he is writing concerning this dictator – 'the man of sin.' See verses 1-4: 'Now we beseech you, brethren, by the coming of our Lord Jesus Christ, and by our gathering together unto Him, that ye be not soon shaken in mind, or be troubled, neither by spirit, nor by word, nor by letter as from us, as that the day of Christ is at hand. Let no man deceive you by any means: for *that day shall not come,* except there come a falling away first, and that man of sin be revealed, the son of perdition; who opposeth and exalteth himself above all that is called God, or that is worshipped; so that he as God sitteth in the temple of God, shewing himself that he is God.' Notice these words: 'that day shall not come' – the day of the Lord. The Bible makes it quite evident that the manifestation of this world dictator will not be until after the Rapture. Paul speaks of this in 1 Thessalonians 4. His rise to power will be sudden. Just as the Lord Jesus

Christ was kept for thirty years, out of the limelight in Nazareth, and then suddenly brought forward after His baptism at the marriage feast in Cana, so will this dictator suddenly appear.

The Bible also mentions him in Daniel 7:8: 'I considered the horns, and, behold, there came up among them another little horn, before whom there were three of the first horns plucked up by the roots: and, behold, in this horn were eyes like the eyes of a man, and a mouth speaking great things.' He is mentioned again in verse 25 of the same chapter: 'And he shall speak great words against the Most High, and shall wear out the saints of the Most High, and think to change times and laws: and they shall be given into his hand until a time and times and the dividing of time.' He will be virtually all-powerful, but notice the Bible says 'They shall be given into his hand.' Who is the giver? You may ask. God in heaven, Who made the earth and all that therein is. He is the Giver! In Daniel 8 the Dictator is mentioned again, in fuller detail, in verses 23 to 25. 'And in the latter time of their kingdom, when the transgressors are come to the full, a king of fierce countenance, and understanding dark sentences, shall stand up. And his power shall be mighty, but not by his own power: And he shall destroy wonderfully, and shall prosper, and practise, and shall destroy the mighty and the holy people. And through his policy also he shall cause craft to prosper in his hand; and he shall magnify himself in his heart, and by peace shall destroy many: he shall also stand up against the Prince of princes; but he shall be broken without hand.' Also in chapter 11: 36-45. There we see that while he is in power he will conquer every one of his foes. Verse 40: 'And at the time of the end shall the king of the south push at him: and the king of the north shall come against him like a whirlwind, with chariots, and with horsemen, and with many ships; and he shall enter into the countries, and shall overflow and pass over.'

This dictator will not only reign. He will assume deity to himself. In Daniel 11:38 we read 'In his estate shall he honour the God of forces: and a god whom his fathers knew not shall he honour with gold, and silver, and with precious stones, and pleasant things.' Evidently, he will present himself as the god to be worshipped – a god of the forces of nature – and he will prove it with signs and wonders. This is what Paul means when he says he 'opposeth and exalteth himself above all that is called God, or that is worshipped; so that he as god sitteth in the temple of God, shewing himself that he is God' (2 Thessalonians 2:4). The Lord Jesus Christ referred to this when He said in Matthew 24:15-16, 'When ye therefore shall see the abomination of desolation, spoken of by Daniel the prophet, stand in the holy place, then let them which be in Judaea flee into the mountains.' And what, you may ask, is his name? The Bible speaks of him as the Beast, but also as the Antichrist. He is the dictator who will rule over political Babylon. And how long will he reign? His reign will be brief. He will not be revealed until after the Rapture of the Church. The period of seven years which follows this is usually called The Great Tribulation, and it is during this period that he will reign. In Revelation 19:19-20, we read of his end – in battle with the Lord Jesus Christ when He returns to reign over this earth: 'And I saw the beast, and the kings of the earth, and their armies, gathered together to make war against him that sat on the horse, and against his army. And the beast was taken, and with him the false prophet that wrought miracles before him, with which he deceived them that had received the mark of the beast, and them that worshipped his image. These both were cast alive into a lake of fire burning with brimstone.'

ITS DEVASTATION

The Book of Revelation is indeed as its title indicates, a Revelation – a revelation of God's plan for the future. In this chapter we have thought of political Babylon in relation to its desire, which we have seen is unity – unity without Christ, and therefore on a rotten foundation. Secondly, we have considered its dictator, and now lastly we must see revealed in God's Word its devastation.

Political Babylon will not last for long! It is to be destroyed, completely. The second verse of Revelation 18 says 'He cried mightily with a strong voice, saying, Babylon the great is fallen, is fallen, and is become the habitation of devils, and the hold of every foul spirit, and a cage of every unclean and hateful bird.' This ungodly federation of nations under the control of its dictator – the Antichrist – is to be smashed. Its devastation will be complete. Satan's plan to have a world church in Ecclesiastical Babylon and a world federation of nations in Political Babylon will be thwarted just at the moment it seems to be succeeding. God will intervene in the affairs of men and will pour out His judgments. In verse 8 we learn that *in one day* God will smash this system: 'Therefore shall her plagues come in one day, death, and mourning, and famine; and she shall be utterly burned with fire: for strong is the Lord God who judgeth her.' Men and women the world over will lament the end of Political Babylon. Kings and rulers, merchants and sailors and others will bewail her. In heaven, however, there will be a very different scene – a scene of great rejoicing. Verses 20 and 21 read 'Rejoice over her, thou heaven, and ye holy apostles and prophets; for God hath avenged you on her. And a mighty angel took up a stone like a great millstone, and cast it into the sea, saying, Thus with violence shall that great city Babylon be thrown down, and shall be found no more at all.'

This devastation of Political Babylon will take place about seven years after the Rapture of the Church. The Antichrist will have broken his promises of peace to the Jews, and will be leading vast armies to exterminate Israel for ever. The Bible tells us in Isaiah 10:28-32 of the approach of these armies. 'He is come to Aiath, he is passed to Migron; at Michmash he hath laid up his carriages: they are gone over the passage: they have taken up their lodging at Geba; Ramah is afraid; Gibeah of Saul is fled. Lift up thy voice, O daughter of Gallim: cause it to be heard unto Laish, O poor Anathoth. Madmenah is removed; the inhabitants of Gebim gather themselves to flee. As yet shall he remain at Nob that day: he shall shake his hand against the mount of the daughter of Zion, the hill of Jerusalem.'

The people will be alarmed by signs which they shall see – signs which the Lord Jesus Christ mentions in Matthew 24:29-30: 'Immediately after the tribulation of those days shall the sun be darkened, and the moon shall not give her light, and the stars shall fall from heaven, and the powers of the heavens shall be shaken: And then shall appear the sign of the Son of man in heaven: and then shall all the tribes of the earth mourn, and they shall see the Son of man coming in the clouds of heaven with power and great glory.' Most of them will have gathered in the valley of Megiddo, which is west of the River Jordan and in the plain of Jezreel, ready for the final attack on Jerusalem. In Revelation 16:16 we read that the sixth angel of judgment 'gathered them together into a place called in the Hebrew tongue Armageddon.' This will be the place of God's appointing for the devastation of Political Babylon. In Zechariah 14:2 and 3 we have yet another prophecy concerning this: 'For I will gather all nations against Jerusalem to battle; and the city shall be taken, and the houses rifled, and the women ravished; and half of the city shall go forth into captivity, and the residue of the people shall not be cut off from the city. Then shall the Lord go forth, and fight against those nations, as when He fought in the day of battle.' The Lord Himself will lead forth the armies of heaven to destroy the Antichrist, the False Prophet and their political system. The Bible mentions this in other places too. (E.g. Isaiah 63:1-6).

The end of this great system, which Satan had planned and which will apparently succeed for a time, is sure to come. The Bible says so! And the Bible is true! The return of the Lord Jesus Christ in power and glory will mark the end. The Antichrist and his hosts will be smashed at the great battle of Armageddon. In Revelation 19:11-21 we have a preview. This great world system – Political Babylon, like Ecclesiastical Babylon will be smashed to atoms. The King is coming!

CONCLUSION

In conclusion, let us return to the scene in heaven. There, we see great rejoicing over the fall of Babylon. And who are those who are rejoicing? The chief ones will be those who compose the Church – the True Church. During the Great Tribulation the Church will be in heaven and every Christian will appear before the Judgment Seat of Christ. Some will be ashamed, for they have wasted their lives. Others will receive great rewards for service accomplished here on earth. How will it be with you, my friend? How tragic it will be for some Christians to stand there and see positions which might have been theirs going to others, because perhaps they have indulged in worldly pleasures, or even just wasted their time. At that Judgment Seat we shall have to give an account of the way we have used our time, our talents and our money. Let us search our hearts and lives now, and put them in order while we yet have time. Thank God we shall miss the Great Tribulation because the Church will be caught up first, but we may miss receiving rewards! Will you miss yours? Perhaps God has been speaking to you and today for the first time you have realised that judgment is coming. Perhaps you never before thought of unsaved friends or loved ones who will be there when judgment falls. Will you not now dedicate or perhaps re-dedicate your life completely to the Lord Jesus Christ? Ask Him to take complete control, and to use you mightily until the moment of His return.

CHAPTER SIXTEEN
THE WEDDING OF THE AGES

Reading: Revelation 19:1-16

Text: Revelation 19:7: 'The marriage of the Lamb is come, and His wife hath made herself ready.'

INTRODUCTION

Heaven's great wedding! Yes, this is not too far away! In fact, it is due very shortly! Most people are interested in weddings. Many like to attend them and watch them. This one is a wedding we can attend ourselves – provided we are suitable. And how do we know if we are suitable or not? The answer simply is this: *Are we saved?* Do we belong to the Bridegroom? Have we a right to be there? No gate-crashers will be allowed. This occasion will be fabulous beyond compare. 'The marriage of the Lamb is come.'

ANTICIPATED IN HEAVEN

Notice, first of all, that this marriage is anticipated in heaven. Yes, it will be the greatest event since Calvary when the Lord Jesus Christ made full atonement for our sins. No simple language will be able to adequately describe the occasion. The weddings of royalty and other famous people will fade into insignificance in contrast with the Marriage of the Lamb.

Perhaps someone is asking who the Lamb is. Who is this Bridegroom? We have the answer in John 1:29 where John the Baptist said 'Behold the Lamb of God which taketh away the sin of the world.' It is none other than the Lord

Jesus Christ! He is the Lamb of God! Many passages of Scripture call Him this. Much Old Testament teaching referred to Him – telling their readers that there would be a Lamb coming who would make atonement for sin, and that Lamb was Christ the Lord. The New Testament reveals how He was conceived supernaturally, and born in Bethlehem, how He lived, how He preached, how He touched people's lives, and how He chose to go to the Cross and give His life a ransom for sinners. As 1 Timothy 1:15 says: 'Christ Jesus came into the world to save sinners.' May I ask, friend, are *you* saved? Are you ready for this great wedding?

This great wedding is anticipated in heaven, for it will mark the union of the heavenly Bridegroom with His Bride which is the Church – that body of saved people. It is not 'church' people or religious people, or people who are kind and do good works. No. It is only those who have repented of their sins, and been cleansed in the precious blood of the Saviour. Is that your condition?

In 2 Corinthians 11:2, the apostle Paul writes to Christians and this is what he says: 'I have espoused you to one Husband, that I may present you as a chaste virgin to Christ.' In other words, once we are saved, we are part of the Bride of Christ. We are 'engaged' – fully committed to being His for ever.

This wedding certainly is anticipated in heaven. The Lord Jesus Christ laid aside His splendour and glory for 33 years that He might obtain His Bride. He returned to heaven and today He is waiting on the last person to be saved to complete His Bride. Would you, my unsaved friend, perhaps be that last person? When the Bride is complete or ready He will come and get her. The trumpet will sound. The Lord Jesus will come to the air and all who are saved – from all over the world – will suddenly and silently ascend to meet the Saviour! What a hope! And the angels in heaven must be anticipating that moment all the time! Yes, indeed, this event is anticipated in heaven! 'The marriage of the Lamb is come, and His wife hath made herself ready.' Secondly, the Bridegroom is:-

THE WEDDING OF THE AGES

APPRECIATED IN PERSON

In the first part of an Eastern wedding there is the betrothal or engagement. The second part is the presentation of the Bride to the Bridegroom. That is the moment when they become legally married.

In Ephesians 5:25 we read 'Christ loved the church, and gave Himself for it.' Galatians 2:20 states that 'the Son of God loved me and gave Himself for me.' In Revelation 1:5 John speaks of 'Him that loved us, and washed us from our sins in His blood.' Do you, my friend, appreciate the fact that the Saviour left heaven and went to the Cross that you and I might have life – eternal life? The Lord's own people can sometimes forget this fact.

The day is fast approaching when the Rapture of the Church will take place and we shall be presented to our Saviour. We shall behold Him Who was nailed to the tree for us! In Old Testament times the Jews had to take a lamb at the time of the Passover. It had to be put to death. Its blood was shed, and this was a picture of the coming Lamb of God Who would make atonement for our sins. All who were under the shelter of the blood of the lamb were safe in the day of judgment, and all today who are under the blood of the Lamb of God are safe – safe for ever!

Do you, do I, really appreciate what the Saviour has done for us? Are you looking forward to seeing Him – to meeting Him, to being with Him for ever and ever?

Appreciated in Person. Yes, He will be indeed most appreciated by many of us. We shall behold the One Who loved us poor sinners so much that He went to the Cross to pay the price for us and set us free eternally. But, some believers are not living as they should be. Some will certainly be embarrassed when the Lord returns and finds them doing wrong deeds. Some Christians will only get into heaven by the grace of God, and the fact that they did trust the Lord as their personal Saviour. Is there someone reading this like that perhaps? Friend, you can make a fresh start today and live for the Lord Jesus Christ daily! Paul says in Ephesians 5:27 that He intends to 'present to Himself a glorious church, not having spot, or wrinkle, or any such thing; but that it should be holy and without blemish.' Christian friend, we need to live holy lives – lives that will not bring disgrace on the name of our Saviour.

On that glorious day, the day of the wedding of the ages, the Bride of Christ will be perfect, for we shall be covered with the robe of His righteousness. As the Bible says in 1 Corinthians 15:51 'We shall be changed, in a moment, in the twinkling of an eye.' And what a blessing that is, for some of us do need changing!

The solemn fact is that before we attend this great wedding, every Christian will go before the Judgment Seat of Christ, to be examined for their lives, not their souls. Those who live for the Saviour will be rewarded, and those who live for self will see their rewards going elsewhere. Salvation is ours by grace. Rewards will only be for service and faithfulness.

'The marriage of the Lamb is come, and His wife hath made herself ready.' This verse leads us on to another thought. The Bridegroom will be:-

ADORED IN PRACTICE

Yes, friend, the Lord Jesus Christ, the Heavenly Bridegroom, will be adored in practice. Have we not often sung at Christmas the words of the hymn:-

Oh, come let us adore Him,
Oh, come let us adore Him;
Oh, come let us adore Him;
Christ, the Lord.

What exactly has that meant to you – to me? Do we really adore Him? The Bible says 'Christ was once offered to bear the sins of many' (Hebrews 9:28), you and me! He left all His eternal glory and came to earth to redeem men, women, boys and girls. He went to Calvary and yielded up His life, shedding His precious, sinless blood that we might be saved. Friends, we need to adore Him. We need to praise Him and worship Him.

Adored in practice. Yes, by humans and by angels!

THE WEDDING OF THE AGES

Jesus my Saviour to Bethlehem came;
Born in a manger to sorrow and shame:
Oh, it was wonderful! Blest be His name!
Seeking for me, for me!

In heaven, those there worship the Saviour. Revelation 4:10,11 tells us 'The four and twenty elders fall down before Him that sat on the throne, and worship Him that liveth for ever and ever, and cast their crowns before the throne, saying, Thou art worthy, O Lord, to receive glory and honour and power.' In the following chapter, in describing the angels, John tells us that millions of them cry out 'Worthy is the Lamb that was slain to receive power and riches, and wisdom, and strength, and honour, and glory and blessing.'

Surely, we who love the Lord ought to worship Him and praise His holy name daily. We ought to adopt a spirit of constant worship and praise in our hearts! If we do that, Christian friend, we will not be miserable. We won't grumble! As Paul says in Romans 8:37, we shall be 'more than conquerors through Him that loved us.'

The third stage in an Eastern wedding is Celebration. The first is Betrothal, the second is Presentation and the third is Celebration. This has nothing to do with meetings which are called 'celebrations.' That is a complete misnomer. We attend meetings to worship God and to hear the Gospel. We have nothing of ourselves to celebrate, for we are all sinful. However, we can and should have a spirit of praise, for our Saviour left heaven for us. He shed His blood for us. He died for us, and He is coming again *for us.*

'The marriage of the Lamb is come, and His wife hath made herself ready.' The Marriage Supper is going to be a tremendous occasion. Every believer from all the centuries will be present. We could call that occasion the Wedding Reception. The Lord Jesus was once at one of these occasions, in Cana of Galilee. His presence there made the feast! Revelation 19:9 says 'Blessed are they which are called unto the marriage supper of the Lamb.' Can I ask, friend, are you one who has been called? If not, then the Holy Spirit is calling you now to repent and trust the Saviour, and thus be ready! Will you do that NOW?

In the opening verses of Matthew 25, the Lord Jesus describes His coming and how there were ten virgins who were supposed to be watching for the coming of the Bridegroom. Five were ready, but the others were not. They were rejected permanently. The Lord said to these religious people 'I know you not', and they were turned away. Jesus went on to say 'Watch therefore, for ye know neither the day nor the hour wherein the Son of Man cometh.' How important it is to be ready! Jesus may come at any moment, and if you are not saved today, tomorrow would then be too late. The Bible says 'Now is the day of salvation.'

The Lord Jesus Christ will certainly be adored in practice. Every saved soul will wish to see and praise Him for saving their never-dying souls. As the hymn writer put it, we shall sing:-

> Oh how I love Him, how I adore Him,
> My breath, my sunshine, my all in all!
> The great Creator became my Saviour,
> And all God's fullness dwelleth in Him.

'The marriage of the Lamb is come, and His wife hath made herself ready.' Let us look finally at the Lamb:-

ACCLAIMED IN POWER AND GLORY

There is a day coming when the Lamb of God is going to come to this earth and then He will be acclaimed in power and glory. Seven years after He comes to the air, He is returning to rule over this whole earth for a thousand years. In heaven, the judgment Seat of Christ will be past. The Marriage Supper of the Lamb will be over. On the earth, the coming world ruler – the Antichrist – will have gathered the world's armies in Israel for the world's final battle. Armageddon will be a terrible reality. The plain of Megiddo will be covered with millions of soldiers, and poor Israel will think all is lost.

THE WEDDING OF THE AGES

Suddenly the heavens will open, and, as John tells us in Revelation 19:11-14, 'Behold a white horse; and He that sat upon him was called Faithful and True, and in righteousness He doth judge and make war . . . And the armies which were in heaven followed Him upon white horses.' The Lamb of God, the Lord Jesus Christ, will then be coming to conquer and reign. As King of kings and Lord of lords, the Lord Jesus will conquer, defeat and destroy the armies of the nations. The Antichrist and False Prophet will be sent to the Lake of Fire to be tormented for ever and ever, and Jesus shall reign over the whole world for one thousand years. His heavenly Bride will be with Him, and all His enemies will bow before Him. As Philippians 2:10 says: 'Every knee shall bow.'

Acclaimed in power and glory. Yes, indeed, the Lord Jesus, the once rejected One, will be truly acclaimed. As He descends to the Mount of Olives from where He left nearly two thousand years ago, Israel will acclaim their looked-for Messiah. The people of the world will see the King of all the earth take His rightful power and place. The peace that the nations seek will at last be established. The curse will be lifted and the animal creation will become completely tame. Zechariah 14:16 tells us 'It shall come to pass, that every one that is left of all the nations which came against Jerusalem shall even go up from year to year to worship the King, the Lord of hosts.' Those who don't go to worship will have no rain and will be punished with plagues. Just think of it. All Muslims and everyone else who is against Israel and the Lord Jesus will simply *have* to worship Him and acclaim Him in power and glory. And, praise the Lord, His Bride will be there to see it all! Will YOU, my friend, be with Him as part of His Bride, or will you be compelled to worship Him? Today, you can repent and trust Him as your personal Saviour. The Bible says in Acts 16:31 'Believe on the Lord Jesus Christ and thou shalt be saved.' Today is your opportunity to be saved. Don't miss it, friend, and end up lost for ever.

CONCLUSION

The Wedding of the Ages! Yes, it will surely be that. God the Father will be there. The Bridegroom, the Lord Jesus Christ, the Lamb of God, will be the centre. His Bride, covered by the robe of His righteousness, will be at His side. The guests, all the Old Testament believers, called in Scripture 'the friends of the Bridegroom', they will be there. And myriads of angels will watch the scene. But, will YOU be there? All are invited, for the Bible says again and again 'Whosoever shall call upon the name of the Lord shall be saved.' The invitations to this great wedding go out to everyone. But there is only one way in which we can be there. We must repent of our sin and ask the Lord to save us and cleanse us with His precious blood.

Christ alone can save. Crucified, risen, exalted and coming again, He alone can save. The Bible says 'Neither is there salvation in any other, for there is none other name under heaven given among men, whereby we must be saved.' Will you trust the Saviour NOW?

> Have you any room for Jesus,
> He, Who bore your load of sin?
> As He knocks and asks admission,
> Sinner, will you let Him in?
> Room for Jesus, King of Glory,
> Hasten now, His Word obey;
> Swing the heart's door widely open,
> Bid Him enter while you may.

CHAPTER SEVENTEEN
ARMAGEDDON

Reading: Revelation 19:11-21

Text: Revelation 16:16: 'And He gathered them together into a place called in the Hebrew tongue Armageddon.'

INTRODUCTION

The word 'Armageddon' conjures up many different pictures in the mind. People in the world who know very little about God's Word seem to know about Armageddon. It speaks to many of blood and battle, of death and finality, and this is correct! The Battle of Armageddon is to be the greatest battle and blood-bath ever seen here on earth. This is to be the place where God will deal in judgment with the nations because of their persecution of Israel and because of their own sinfulness.

People today seem to think that they can campaign against nuclear war, and atomic and other devilish bombs, but their protests are futile, for the Bible clearly states that Armageddon is ahead. It *must* come and millions of soldiers will perish in this, the world's greatest war. 'And HE gathered them together into a place called in the Hebrew tongue Armageddon.' When God gathers, no one can stop Him! Let me ask you, right away, are you saved, or is Armageddon your prospect?

Let us look first of all at:-

THE PLACE

Where is the place? You will find it on the edge of the Plain of Esdraelon in Israel. It is a vast arena, a great flat plain, where Israel fought many battles long ago, and it is here that the world's greatest battle, the Battle of Armageddon, will be fought. It is west of the River Jordan, about ten miles south of Nazareth, and fifteen miles inland from the Mediterranean. Here it was that Deborah and Barak fought and defeated the Canaanites (see Judges 4 and 5). Gideon also had a great victory here and Saul was killed in battle on this great plain. We could mention others also, but space forbids.

Armageddon, or Megiddo, is on the plain of Esdraelon, and on this plain also have fought the Crusaders, Saracens, Turks, Arabs and warriors from many nations. It seems from the Bible that this Battle of Armageddon will stretch from the plain of Megiddo to Jerusalem. Joel 3:2 and 12 speak of the 'valley of Jehoshaphat.' The Bible says 'I will also gather all nations, and will bring them down into the valley of Jehoshaphat.' In Zechariah 14:2 we also see that Jerusalem itself is involved – 'I will gather all nations against Jerusalem to battle; and the city shall be taken, and the houses rifled, and the women ravished.' Isaiah 34 and 63 also picture the Lord Jesus returning with blood stained garments from Edom, which is in the South of Israel.

So, where is the place? We can safely conclude that while the battle will centre on the plain of Megiddo, the whole campaign of Armageddon will likely cover a great part of Israel.

Now, let us look briefly at:-

THE PARTICIPANTS

Our text says 'And He gathered them together into a place called in the Hebrew tongue Armageddon.' Who, we ask, are the people referred to as 'them'? Dr John F. Walvoord, in one of his books, says 'The dramatic conclusion of the 'times of the Gentiles' is described in prophecy as a gigantic world war which is climaxed by the second coming of Christ. The war that brings to a close the times of the Gentiles, which has already embraced 2500 years of history, is also the final effort of Satan in his strategy of opposition to the divine program of God. The second coming of Christ is God's answer.'

The situation is this. Long ago, God promised His earthly people, Israel, the land which Israel now occupies, and far beyond its present borders. However, the Arabs and Russians and many others would dearly like to have possession of it and control over the whole of the Middle East. But when God promises something, He keeps His Word, and Israel will get the whole territory promised! Now, who will be the participants in this final great conflict? We find from the Bible that in the end times, during the later part of the Great Tribulation period, the Antichrist will reign over the whole world. Revelation 13:7 says, 'Power was given him over all kindreds, and tongues and nations.' He will be in supreme control.

However, the Bible also tells us that there will be at that time four great world powers. There will be, firstly, the ten-kingdom federation in Europe, ruled by the Beast or Antichrist. Then, there will be the Northern confederation of Russia and her satellites. The Bible then speaks of the kings of the East, namely China and the hordes from the East, and finally, the king of the South. This will no doubt be the Arab nations. There will be one more Power, the Lord Jesus Christ and His mighty army from heaven. They will come in to finalise matters and defeat the enemy and destroy him.

It would seem from the Bible that these four earthly groups will be fighting each other, and also God and His earthly people. Zechariah 12:2-3 says, 'Behold, I will make Jerusalem a cup of trembling unto all the people round about, when they shall be in the siege both against Judah and against Jerusalem. And in that day will I make Jerusalem a burdensome stone for all people: all that burden themselves with it shall be cut in pieces, though all the people of the earth be gathered together against it.' From this Scripture, it is clear that the whole world will be the participant.

If you are not saved, my friend, you may be involved in this, that is, if you are still alive, for millions are to perish in the Great Tribulation judgments before Armageddon occurs. You can repent of your sin now and ask the Lord Jesus to save you, if you will! Without Him as your Saviour, you are lost.

> There is a fountain filled with blood,
> Drawn from Immanuel's veins,
> And sinners plunged beneath that flood
> Lose all their guilty stains.
> The dying thief rejoiced to see
> That fountain in his day;
> And there may I, though vile as he,
> Wash all my sins away.

Trust the Saviour NOW, before it is too late!

THE PURPOSE

Our text says 'And HE gathered them together into a place called in the Hebrew tongue Armageddon.' What is the purpose of this final, great conflict?

As we examine the Word of God we find things become quite clear! God has His Own plans, and although man at times may feel that things are getting out of hand, He is yet working things out as He wishes. Revelation 16 and many other Scriptures also make it clear that the Lord is going to gather all His enemies to Israel, to Armageddon, in order to destroy them! Man is naturally rebellious and during the previous few years man will have been worshipping a Satanic creature. The Bible says in Revelation 13:3, 'all the world wondered after the beast.' In verse 4 of the same chapter it says 'And they worshipped the dragon (Satan) which gave power unto the beast: and they worshipped the beast.' So, the world will be openly worshipping Satan and his representative, the Man of Sin.

In Revelation 16:13-14 we read, 'I saw three unclean spirits like frogs come out of the mouth of the dragon, and out of the mouth of the beast, and out of the mouth of the false prophet. For they are the spirits of devils, working miracles, which go forth unto the kings of the earth and of the whole world, to gather them to the battle of that great day of God almighty.' So, we find that God uses this means to draw the whole world to battle at Armageddon. Satan knows that Christ will be returning and his armies of the world will oppose and fight Him. Armageddon is a plain, 14 miles wide and 20 miles long, so there will be room here alone for millions of men and much equipment. But the war will cover the whole land, probably about two hundred miles from top to bottom.

The purpose? War, opposition to God and His earthly people, Israel. Possibly too, there may be some desire on the part of the Chinese, or Russians, or Arabs to conquer and rule the world, but that is incidental. God will be gathering the forces Himself, for His purposes! The word used by God regarding 'battle' in the Greek really means 'campaign.' So we find that Armageddon is not a single battle, but a campaign.

Daniel 11 tells something of the battle or campaign of Armageddon. Verse 36 tells us that the Antichrist will 'magnify himself above every god, and shall speak marvellous things against the God of gods, and shall prosper till the indignation (Tribulation) be accomplished.' Verse 40 of this same chapter says 'At the time of the end shall the king of the south push at him: and the king of the north shall come against him like a whirlwind, with chariots, and with horsemen, and with many ships; and he shall enter into the countries, and shall overflow and pass over.' The same chapter says that Egypt will be overthrown. The Libyans and the Ethiopians (both today Communist sympathisers at least) will be following. Daniel 11:44 says 'Tidings out of the east, and out of the north shall trouble him: therefore he shall go forth with great fury to destroy.' Revelation 9:16 tells of an army of 200 million coming from the Far East. We happen to know that China today has openly stated that she has an army of that exact size, and she also has said that she is willing to lose 200 million to conquer the world! We are living in exciting times, yes, the last days before Jesus returns for His Own! Let me ask you again, are you ready? Are you going to heaven, saved and washed in the precious blood of Jesus? Or are you lost, and going to hell? There is no in-between. We are all either saved or lost. The Bible tells us to repent and trust the Saviour. Remember, He died on the cross at Calvary to make atonement for your sin! Won't you turn to Him now for salvation? The Bible says 'Whosoever shall call on the name of the Lord shall be saved' (Romans 10:13). Will you call, NOW?

Our text says 'And He gathered them together into a place called in the Hebrew tongue Armageddon.' If you do not repent, you may see this awful war.

THE PROSPECT

We have thought of The Place, The Participants, and the Purpose. Now, let us consider finally The Prospect. What is the outcome going to be?

Again, we turn to the wonderful Word of God. The Bible is God's blueprint for the future. We find the Prospect is two-fold. First of all, what is the prospect for the armies of the world? The answer is quite simple: Death and Destruction! Millions of soldiers will be hurled into eternity. Revelation 14:14-20 tell us 'And the angel thrust his sickle into the earth, and gathered the vine of the earth, and cast it into the great winepress of the wrath of God. And the winepress was trodden without the city, (Jerusalem), and blood came out of the winepress, even unto the horses bridles, by the space of a thousand and six hundred furlongs (200 miles).' So, the PROSPECT for the world's armies is a great lake of blood stretching 200 miles. And the Bible tells us in Isaiah 34:3 'their slain shall also be cast out, and their stink shall come up out of their carcases and the mountains shall be melted with their blood.' What a prospect!

But, friend, there is a different prospect. We look now at Revelation 19 and we see the Lord Jesus coming with His heavenly hosts. Verse 11 says 'I saw heaven opened, and behold a white horse; and He that sat upon him was called Faithful and True, and in righteousness He doth judge and make war.'

ARMAGEDDON

This is the Lord Jesus Christ returning in power and in great glory to conquer the rebel millions and set up His Millennial kingdom. Verses 14-16 say 'And the armies which were in heaven followed Him upon white horses, clothed in fine linen, white and clean. And out of His mouth goeth a sharp sword, that with it He should smite the nations: and He shall rule them with a rod of iron: and He treadeth the winepress of the fierceness and wrath of Almighty God. And He hath on His vesture and on His thigh a name written, KING OF KINGS, AND LORD OF LORDS.' As the hymn says:-

> Jesus shall reign where're the sun
> Doth her successive journeys run;
> His kingdom stretch from shore to shore,
> Till moons shall wax and wane no more.

This will be the moment when the Lord Jesus Christ shall openly triumph over Satan, the Antichrist and the False Prophet. Also, He will have subdued all the nations of the earth, and will reign for a thousand years as their supreme Monarch. The prospect for Christ and His followers is *total victory!*

CONCLUSION

'And He gathered them together into a place called in the Hebrew tongue Armageddon.' We have only really touched on the fringe of this great subject, but we have seen enough to know that it will be worse than terrible to be here. When Christ returns it seems that the armies of the world will all die instantly. Revelation 19:20 and 21 tell us, 'And the beast was taken, and with him the false prophet that wrought miracles before him, with which he deceived them that had received the mark of the beast, and them that worshipped his image. These both were cast alive into a lake of fire burning with brimstone. And the remnant were slain with the sword of Him that sat upon the horse, which sword proceeded out of His mouth: and all the fowls were filled with their flesh.'

The time has arrived when these end-time happenings are at the door! Any moment the Lord Jesus may return for His Own, for they will be taken out of the world seven years before Armageddon. Are you ready? Christian, are you living for self, or witnessing for Jesus? Is your life in order? You can put things right NOW.

Unsaved friend, what are you going to do? You can repent of your sin now and be saved, or you can just be indifferent, and then eventually land in hell. Can you see how terrible life is going to be? The air will explode, 100 pound hailstones will fall, earthquakes will be the order of the day. The Bible says 'Flee from the wrath to come.' Will you flee NOW to Jesus? He has promised in His Word 'Him that cometh to Me I will in no wise cast out' (John 6:37). Will you come, now? Christ alone can save, and He will save you, if you ask Him. If you don't, then some day you will meet Him as your Judge. The prospect for all who are not saved is an eternity in hell, the lake of fire. The Bible says 'The blood of Jesus Christ, His Son, cleanseth us from all sin' (1 John 1:7). Ask for that cleansing now.

CHAPTER EIGHTEEN

THE GREAT WHITE THRONE

Reading: Revelation 20

Text: Revelation 20:12: 'I saw the dead, small and great, stand before God; and the books were opened.'

INTRODUCTION

Our text comes toward the end of the Bible. In fact, it is at the close of the third last chapter of the Bible. The chapter commences with the wonderful news that after the battle of Armageddon which is not too far ahead, and at the close of the Great Tribulation which will start after the Lord Jesus Christ returns to the air and takes away His believing people, there is going to be ushered in the millennium – a thousand years of peace and prosperity when Christ will reign supreme over the whole earth. Satan will be chained up for that period. Those martyred for their faith, in the Great Tribulation, and for refusing the mark of the beast, will be raised from the dead to join all the believers who took part in the First Resurrection at the Rapture of the church.

Time passes. The thousand year reign of the Saviour will be through, and in verses 7 and 8 we read 'When the thousand years are expired, Satan shall be loosed out of his prison, and shall go out to deceive the nations.' Man will rebel. Jerusalem will be surrounded, and God will intervene by sending fire from heaven to destroy them. Satan will then be cast – as verse 10 says – 'into the lake of fire and brimstone, where the beast (Antichrist) and false prophet are, and shall be tormented day and night for ever and ever.'

Verse 11 introduces us to the setting up of the Great White Throne of judgment, and this leads us to consider our text in detail. 'I saw the dead, small and great, stand before God; and the books were opened.'

THE RESURRECTION OF THE DEAD

'I saw the dead . . .' *Which dead?* you may be asking. All the true Christians who received the Lord Jesus Christ as their Saviour and were washed in His precious blood will already be alive and with Christ. So, who are these dead people? The answer is simple and plain. All the unsaved from all generations, and from all races and nations, and from all periods of time! They are going to stand before God! Many unconverted people hope that for them death is the end, and may get their bodies cremated hoping to prevent any resurrection. But, God has stated in His infallible Word that every unsaved soul will be raised from the dead to stand before God and be judged. Verse 5 of this chapter says 'The rest of the dead lived not again until after the thousand years were finished.' So, after the Millennial Reign of Christ, and after Satan's rebellion, the Lord is going to raise up every dead person who was not saved! No one will be omitted.

Can I ask you, at this point, are YOU saved? Are you born again and washed in the precious blood of the Lamb? If not, you will be raised from the dead for the judgment of the Great White Throne. No one will escape. Your only hope is to repent and trust the Saviour today. As the hymn says:-

Be in time, be in time!

While the voice of Jesus calls you,

Be in time.

'I saw the dead, small and great, stand before God; and the books were opened.' The Resurrection of the Dead will take place and it will not matter one iota whether their bodies were devoured by worms in the grave, by sharks or other fish at sea, or by flames: *all* will be resurrected. It will not simply be a case of the spirits of the dead coming before the Great White Throne. No. They will have their bodies resurrected, bodies in which they rejected God's way of salvation. This resurrection is going to take place and you, my unsaved friend, will be there!

Notice, secondly, our text speaks of:-

THE RIGHTEOUSNESS OF GOD

It is the Righteous One, the only Just One, before whom the lost will stand. The Lord could have appointed someone else to dispose of all those who were lost and undone. However, He chose to oversee this matter Himself. He alone is fully righteous and just, and all who will appear before the Great White Throne will be treated justly and fairly.

'I saw the dead, small and great, stand before God.' People from all walks of life, some important and others with no great position, will stand before God! *He* will be their Judge. *He* will decide their ultimate punishment, although all will be sent to hell! Some people do not believe in hell, but the Word of God speaks more of hell than it does of heaven!

The Lord, Who will be on the Great White Throne, has done all in His power to save men and women, boys and girls, from going to hell. The Bible tells us in John 3:16, 'God so loved the world that He gave His only begotten Son, that whosoever believeth in Him should not perish but have everlasting life.' Several times in different places in the Bible He also says 'Whosoever shall call on the name of the Lord shall be saved.' We can see that the Lord is righteous and just, for His offer of salvation and forgiveness is to whosoever! Any sinner today can avail himself or herself of God's great salvation. In 1 John 5:11,12 we read 'This is the record, that God hath given to us eternal life, and this life is in His Son. He that hath the Son hath life; and he that hath not the Son of God hath not life.' God's salvation is free to all, but all who have rejected that offer or just been indifferent must face the Lord as their Righteous Judge.

Every man, woman and child on this earth from the beginning of creation will stand before the Great White Throne, unless they have trusted the Saviour. People who believe in false religions will all be there. Our religious leaders who never repented and asked the Lord to save them will all be there. The Righteousness of God will see to it that everyone apart from the saved ones will appear. ' I saw the dead, small and great, stand before God; and the books were opened.' Unsaved one, will you repent NOW and ask the Lord Jesus to save you? My father, J. Danson Smith penned these lines:-

> I wonder if you really knew
> That by His death Christ died for you;
> I wonder just what would you do?
> Believe it! Yes, because its true!
> Christ nothing left for us to do!
> He died for me! He died for you!
> One look to Him and all is new!
> Sin's past is blotted from God's view;
> Christ paid it all – for me, for you!

We have looked at The Resurrection of the Dead, also at The Righteousness of God. Now, thirdly, let us consider:-

THE RECORD IN THE BOOKS

Our text reminds us of these books. It says 'The books were opened.' Farther down, in verse 12, we read that 'the dead were judged out of those things which were written in the books, according to their works.' From this we learn that all who will appear at the Great White Throne judgment have already been sentenced to hell, but their works will determine the degree of punishment to which they will be subjected. 'According to their works.' This is important, for the righteousness of God demands that justice will be administered. Christians will be rewarded according to what they do or don't do for the Lord. Paul makes this very clear in 2 Corinthians 5:10 where he says 'We (believers) must all appear before the judgment seat of Christ; that every one may receive the things done in his body, according to that he hath done, whether it be good or bad.' Some of the Lord's people will not receive any reward because they are just lazy and don't pray or work for Him.

The unsaved who are bound for an eternity in hell will find their punishment in hell is based on their works. Millions will be in hell who have lived honourable, decent, upright and even religious lives. Their sin is ignoring the Saviour. Luke 12:47 and 48 tell us that those who know the right and do wrong will be tormented far more than those who have less light. In Matthew 7:22 and 23 the Lord Jesus states that 'Many will say to Me in that day, Lord, Lord, have we not prophesied in Thy name? And in Thy name cast out demons? And in Thy name done many wonderful works? And then will I profess unto them, I never knew you: depart from Me, ye that work iniquity.' This Scripture reminds us of so many charismatics who are religious but not saved. Oh, sinner, today I plead with you to repent and ask for the cleansing of the precious blood.

Unsaved friend, let me tell you, God is keeping a full record of your works, and you will be punished on the basis of these. If man has invented the tape recorder many years ago, and more recently the video recorder, how easy it must be for the Lord and His servants to keep a full recording of your life! He has millions of angels – heavenly beings – who serve Him and do His will, and your life and work are being recorded now. You will never be able to deny what is there in the books!

Today is still the Day of Grace. Today, you may repent of your sin and ask the Lord Jesus Christ to save you and cleanse you with His blood. That blood is the only remedy for sin. There is no other! Will you trust the Saviour NOW? Jesus said 'Him that cometh unto Me, I will in no wise cast out' (John 6:37). William Cowper gave us the words of the great hymn:-

> There is a fountain filled with blood,
> Drawn from Immanuel's veins;
> And sinners plunged beneath that flood
> Lose all their guilty stains.
> The dying thief rejoiced to see
> That fountain in his day;
> And there may I, though vile as he,
> Wash all my sins away.

The thief on the cross believed and was saved. Will YOU do that? 'I saw the dead, small and great, stand before God; and the books were opened.'

THE RETRIBUTION FOR THE LOST

We come now to our final thought: Retribution for the Lost. Yes, punishment is coming! Someone may ask how a God of love can do such a thing. The answer is very simple. He saw man's desperate need and sent His only begotten Son into the world to pay the price of man's sin, and all who reject or are simply indifferent or perhaps choose to go their own way must bear the consequences. God the Father gave His best, for you and for me. John 3:17 says 'For God sent not His Son into the world to condemn the world; but that the world through Him might be saved.' In 1 Timothy 1:15 we read 'Christ Jesus came into the world to save sinners.' Romans 5:8 states 'God commendeth His love toward us in that while we were yet sinners Christ died for us.' God's love is real. He saw man was in danger of an eternity in hell and He did all He could to save us from going there. Men and women, boys and girls are going to hell by their own choice, and for all the millions of years to come they will remember the various opportunities they had to accept the Saviour.

These words from our text – 'the books were opened' – are most significant. Picture the scene. Standing before the Great White Throne your Judge will open the book of your life and all the records will be revealed. Sentence will then be passed on you as to how severe your torment will be in hell. The

THE GREAT WHITE THRONE

next person is called and on it will go until every unsaved soul is finally dealt with. And, no one will be able to dispute with the Judge that His sentence is unfair. The lake of fire awaits every unbeliever. God never intended men and women to go to hell, for He created that place for the devil and his angels who rebelled, but those who refuse the way of escape are doomed for retribution. As the Lord Jesus Himself said 'I am the Way, the Truth and the Life; no man cometh unto the Father but by Me' (John 14:6). *He* is the only way.

CONCLUSION

In closing this very solemn chapter, may I draw your attention to the last verse in Revelation 20. Here it says 'Whosoever was not found written in the book of life was cast into the lake of fire.' This is a reference to another book, the Lamb's book of life. In it are the names of every soul who has put their trust in the Saviour. All the saved ones are listed there. My name is there! Is yours? If not, it can be today, if you will repent this very moment and seek the cleansing of the precious blood of the Lord Jesus. If you don't you may be rejecting the Lord Jesus for the very last time, and you will end up in hell, remembering all through eternity the various opportunities when you could have been saved. *Today* is the day of salvation. Repent and cry out to the Lord for His salvation *now*. 'Believe on the Lord Jesus Christ and thou shalt be saved' (Acts 16:31).

> Redemption! Oh wonderful story –
> Glad message for you and for me:
> That Jesus has purchased our pardon
> And paid all the debt on the tree.
> Believe it, Oh sinner, believe it;
> Receive the glad message – 'tis true;
> Trust now in the crucified Saviour –
> Salvation He offers to you.

CHAPTER NINETEEN

THE NEW HEAVEN AND THE NEW EARTH

Reading: Revelation 21:1-8

Text: Revelation 21:1: 'I saw a new heaven and a new earth.'

INTRODUCTION

Revelation 21 introduces us to several new things. There is a new heaven and a new earth, a new people, a new Jerusalem, a new temple and a new light. This chapter follows chapter 20, where we find Satan sent to his destiny in the lake of fire. The Great White Throne judgment of all the unsaved will be past, and all these lost souls will have been sent to their final doom in the Lake of Fire where they will abide for ever and ever. This place of unending torment was prepared for Satan and all the angels who rebelled against God. It was not intended for human beings, but all who reject the Lord Jesus Christ, or are simply indifferent to Him, will go there for all the ages to come. What a prospect! If someone reading this is not saved, then repent now of all your sin and put your trust in the Lord Jesus Christ for salvation. He went to the Cross of Calvary to prevent us going to the lake of fire.

Our text is in verse 1, the words of John: 'I saw a new heaven and a new earth.' We must notice first of all:-

THE PASSING

The same verse tells us 'the first heaven and the first earth were passed away.' One day, more than a thousand years from now, this world of ours as we know it will pass away. God says it in His Word, and that is enough. Things will not go on and on for ever as we know them. There is a change coming. Yes, the passing will be a reality. The Lord cannot allow a sin-cursed world to continue. He cleansed it once by a world-wide flood, and promised that He would never use water again in such a judgment. This world of ours is going to be cleansed by fire. The Bible says so. 2 Peter 3:6 and 7 state 'The world that then was, being overflowed with water, perished: But the heavens and the earth, which are now, by the same word are kept in store, reserved unto fire.' Verse 10 of the same chapter states 'The heavens shall pass away with a great noise, and the elements shall melt with fervent heat, the earth also and the works that are therein shall be burned up.'

This word 'heavens' refers to the atmosphere around the world, the place where the birds fly. It is not the stellar heavens where the stars are, just simply what surrounds our world. The passing is the first thing to note, for the Lord is going to cleanse the earth and remake it. He cannot allow a sin-cursed place to continue without a complete clean-out. This fire will cleanse the world but not destroy it. The world will be rebuilt, and it will be re-inhabited.

So much for the passing. Notice next:-

THE PRESENCE

In the new creation there will be a special presence. Revelation 21:3 says 'I heard a great voice out of heaven saying, Behold, the tabernacle of God is with men, and He will dwell with them, and they shall be His people, and God Himself shall be with them.' This is a wonderful promise. The presence of God the Father will be here on the re-created earth. Back in Isaiah 65:17 we find these words of promise: 'Behold, I create new heavens and a new earth: and the former shall not be remembered, nor come into mind.'

THE NEW HEAVEN AND THE NEW EARTH 161

In the re-created world it seems that God the Father will join His Son, the Lord Jesus Christ, and dwell on earth. At present He remains in the third heaven, or heaven of heavens, no doubt the place where the Lord Jesus Christ is preparing many mansions for His followers. During His millennial reign, when the Lord Jesus controls the whole world, He will eventually hand over all to His Father, and then the Father will presence Himself on the earth. After the cleansing by fire, there will be no more sea. At present three quarters of this world of ours is covered by water, but in the new order the sea will not be needed. Things will probably return to the Edenic conditions when there was no rain and probably no sea either. Water was provided in other ways.

How marvellous and wonderful it will be for the presence of God to be felt. We can feel His presence at times, but it is the Holy Spirit's presence we are aware of. The Lord Jesus said 'He that hath seen me hath seen the Father' (John 14:9). The Bible also says 'The Father sent the Son to be the Saviour of the world' (1 John 4:14). We can never forget the words of John 3:16, 'For God so loved the world that He gave His only begotten Son, that whosoever believeth in Him should not perish but have everlasting life.' Can I ask here, do YOU have this life? If not, you are lost and on the road to hell. Look to the Lord Jesus now, friend, and then you can say with the hymn writer:-

> Simply trusting Thee, Lord Jesus,
> I behold Thee as Thou art;
> And Thy love so pure, so changeless,
> Satisfies my heart.

'I saw a new heaven and a new earth.' Yes, there will be The Passing, also the Presence. Thirdly, in verse 4, we find:-

THE PROVISION

This verse states 'God shall wipe away all tears from their eyes; and there shall be no more death, neither sorrow, nor crying, neither shall there by any more pain: for the former things are passed away.' How wonderful! Everyone on the new earth will live for ever! Death always brings sadness and mourning. Serious sickness also brings death, but in the new creation there will be no sickness either. No pain too is a great promise. All of us suffer pain at times, some people more so than others, but in the new order there will definitely be no pain. The child of God will find full provision made for them. We shall be with our Saviour for all eternity. When He reigns on the earth, we shall reign with Him. When we have needs, these needs will be met. In Leviticus 26:12 we read 'I will walk among you, and will be your God, and ye shall be My people.' In the previous verse we find these words: 'I will set My tabernacle among you.' The presence of God will be adequate provision for every believer. We shall never be hungry. We shall never be ill. We shall never go short of anything, and even today the true Christian has the Lord's promise of provision. 'My God shall supply all your need' (Philippians 4: 19).

The great Bible teacher, Clarence Larkin, speaking of the provision says this: 'the earth shall also put on its Edenic beauty and glory. There shall no longer be thorns and thistles, no parasites or destructive insects, and labour shall be a delight. No serpents shall hiss among its flowers, nor savage beasts lie in ambush to destroy and devour. Its sod shall not be heaped with newly made graves, nor its soil moistened with tears of sorrow and shame, or saturated with human blood. The meek shall inherit the earth, and from North to South, and from East to West, it shall blossom like the rose and be clothed with the verdure of Paradise Restored.' What a prospect. 'I saw a new heaven and a new earth.'

We have considered briefly the Passing, the Presence and the Provision. Now, we may look at:-

THE PROCLAMATION

Yes, the proclamation! What is it? See verse 6: 'I am the Alpha and Omega, the beginning and the end. I will give unto him that is athirst of the fountain of the water of life freely.' What a word! The Lord Jesus Christ is the Be-all

THE NEW HEAVEN AND THE NEW EARTH 163

and the End-all. He is the vital One to know. Do YOU, my friend, know Him. Is He your Saviour? If not, He offers YOU today the water of life freely. What does this mean? He simply is offering you a full and free salvation. The Bible says 'God is not willing that any should perish' (2 Peter 3:9). He has no wish to send people to hell, for He made provision for all to be saved. In Romans 5:6 the Bible says 'Christ died for the ungodly.' It also says in the same chapter 'Christ died for us' (Romans 5:8). Friend, you are included in His death – in the atonement He made on the Cross for sin. But, you have to repent and then accept Him as yours. Will you take that step now and be saved?

There is no other way to heaven. The Lord Jesus said 'I am the door' (John 10:9). The Bible also says in 1 Timothy 1:15, 'Christ Jesus came into the world to save sinners.' We all know that we are sinners, for we are born with that sort of nature, a tendency to sin. Thank God 'the blood of Jesus Christ, His Son, cleanseth us from all sin' (1 John 1:7). The good old hymn invites you:-

Would you be free from your passion and pride?

There's power in the blood, power in the blood;

Come for a cleansing to Calvary's tide,

There's wonderful power in the blood.

Our text says 'I saw a new heaven and a new earth.' The Lord also proclaims 'I am the Alpha and Omega.' These are the first and last letters of the Greek alphabet, and He is simply reminding us that He is the great Creator. John 1:1 says 'In the beginning was the Word.' The Lord was and is the One Who made the earth. He also should be the end or goal. I know Him, but do you? Paul spoke of 'knowing Christ.'

Many years ago a missionary employed a guide to help him cross a desert. When the two men arrived at the edge of the desert, the missionary noticed that there was no road and no track of any kind. All he saw was miles and miles of sand with no footprints anywhere. He turned to his guide and asked 'Where is the road?' The guide gave him a strange look and said quietly 'I am the road.' There is only one road to heaven – and that includes the new heaven and the new earth – and that is the Lord Jesus Christ. In John 14:6 He stated, 'I am the Way, the Truth and the Life; no man cometh to the Father, but by Me.' He is the only way to heaven and home. All other roads lead to hell.

We have one last thought to pass on. It is:-

THE PREVENTION

Yes, the prevention. But of what? Someone may ask. The answer very simply is the prevention of any sinners reaching heaven. God cannot allow sin to spoil the 'new heaven and the new earth.' In verse 8 we read a list of people who will never see heaven unless they repent of their sin and ask the Lord to save them. 'But the fearful, and unbelieving, and the abominable, and murderers, and whoremongers, and sorcerers, and idolaters, and all liars, shall have their part in the lake which burneth with fire and brimstone: which is the second death.' That is clear, is it not? Revelation 21 - which goes on to describe something of the new Jerusalem – finishes with these words: 'There shall in no wise enter into it any thing that defileth, neither whatsoever worketh abomination, or maketh a lie; but they which are written in the Lamb's book of life.' The Lord records the names and details of all who repent of their sin and receive the Lord Jesus Christ into their hearts as their personal Saviour. Do you know if *your* name will be there? If not, now is the moment to repent and ask for His salvation.

Nearly two thousand years ago at Jerusalem, a thief hung on a cross. Next to him was my Saviour, shedding His precious, sinless blood for sinners. That thief looked to Him and trusted Him as his Saviour. He saw no king there, but he had faith to believe, and he put his trust for eternity in Christ. He saw that the Lord was paying the price of his sin. The Philippian jailor also saw his need met when Paul said to him 'Believe on the Lord Jesus Christ, and thou shalt be saved' (Acts 16:31). Zacchaeus, the tax collector, saw in the Lord Jesus the One Who could meet his need of salvation too. Friend, what about you?

THE NEW HEAVEN AND THE NEW EARTH

The story is told of a king who had to deal with a big group of his subjects who rebelled against him. He soon sorted them out with his army, but when things were quiet, he showered them with lavish gifts. When he was asked why he did this, his answer was that he conquered the rebels by power, but now he wanted to win them by love. John 3:16 states 'God so loved the world, that He gave His only begotten Son, that whosoever believeth in Him should not perish but have everlasting life.' Romans 5:8 says 'God commendeth His love toward us in that while we were yet sinners Christ died for us.'

There is no love like the love of Jesus –

Never to fade or fall,

Till into the fold of the peace of God

He has gathered us all.

Jesus' love – precious love,

Boundless and pure and free;

Oh, turn to that love, weary wandering soul:

Jesus pleadeth with thee.

Will you do that now, and be sure of seeing 'The new heaven and the new earth.'

CHAPTER TWENTY
A TREMENDOUS VERSE

Reading: Revelation 21:1-11 and 22-27

Text: Revelation 21:8

INTRODUCTION

This second last chapter of the Bible describes something of the scene after the return of the Lord Jesus Christ to the earth as King of kings and Lord of lords at the close of Armageddon. Antichrist and the armies of the world will have been wiped out, and the millennial reign of the Lord Jesus Christ will have commenced. For the next thousand years this world of ours will know peace – real peace – for the Prince of Peace will be ruling.

Revelation 21 describes something of the New Jerusalem, but verse 8 is interjected, and we read these very solemn words: 'But the fearful, and unbelieving, and the abominable, and murderers, and whoremongers, and sorcerers, and idolaters, and all liars, shall have their part in the lake which burneth with fire and brimstone; which is the second death.'

This text, firstly, deals with:-

AN ENORMOUS COMPANY

Yes, friend, here we have an enormous company of people. Let us look at how the Bible describes them. First of all, we have 'the fearful.' The word used here in the Greek is 'deilos', and it means 'cowardly.' These people are too cowardly to admit that they are sinners who need a Saviour. This is not someone who is afraid. No. The Lord would never send someone to a lost eternity through fear. This is the person who is too cowardly to admit their sin. The Bible reminds us that we are all sinners. 'There is none righteous, no, not one' (Romans 3:10). 'All have sinned and come short of the glory of God' (Romans 3:23). In Romans we are told 'By one man sin entered into the world' (Romans 5:12). Because Adam disobeyed the Lord all of us are born sinners. We have sinful natures – natures which have a natural bias to do wrong. We cannot help this. We simply are poor lost sinners. Good living people may object to being called sinners, but that is what we all are. We may not kill, steal or use bad language, but we still commit sins. Everyone thinks bad thoughts at times. That is sin.

'The fearful.' Is there someone reading this perhaps who is afraid to admit their sinful condition? Come to the Saviour and He will cleanse you and set you free.

Our text goes on to mention another group of people, the 'unbelieving.' Such people do not believe the Word of God, or the word of a faithful preacher of the Gospel. Listen to the words of the Lord Jesus Himself. In John 3:18 He stated, 'He that believeth not is condemned already, because he hath not believed in the name of the only begotten Son of God.' There is only one Saviour, the Lord Jesus Christ. Mohammed cannot save. Mary cannot help either. There is no person anywhere that can save poor, lost sinners, only Jesus. The Bible says in Acts 4:12, 'Neither is there salvation in any other, for there is none other name under heaven given among men whereby we must be saved.' Is there someone reading this who does not believe? You are in danger of hell-fire for all eternity! Repent now and trust the Lord Jesus Christ.

Our text states 'But the fearful, and unbelieving, and the abominable, and murderers, and whoremongers, and sorcerers, and all liars, shall have their part in the lake which burneth with fire and brimstone: which is the second death.' Notice the enormous company.

A TREMENDOUS VERSE

Then see next the word 'abominable.' This reminds us of Genesis 19, where we have the story of Lot and his rescue from Sodom and Gomorrah. In the previous chapter the Lord told Abraham that He was going to wipe out these towns because of their abominations. Today, homosexuality and so on have become noticeable because the government has encouraged it. Such sins are perversions, and in Romans 1:24-29 we learn how God condemns such people and has given them up. That does not mean that they cannot be saved. If they repent of their sin and trust in the precious shed blood of the Lord Jesus, they will be saved. But, without Christ, these people are 'abominable', and they are going to hell.

The next group we read of in this enormous company are referred to as 'murderers.' We live in an age when life has become cheap. There is no more death penalty, so if a murder is committed it only means about seven years in prison if the murderer is caught. There will be no un-forgiven murderers in heaven. Note, *un-forgiven*, for 'the blood of Jesus Christ His Son' can cleanse a murderer as much as one who would like to kill someone. Ernest was a German young man who married a girl and insured her for £100,000. He took her up a hill and threw her over to her death. He was soon caught, and years later in prison he found the Lord Jesus as his Saviour. Now, he is free and an assistant minister of the Gospel. No one is beyond the power of the Gospel.

The enormous company – bound for an eternity in hell. The next word listed here is 'whoremongers.' We need not go on to describe this, but we live in a licentious age where many are quite unfaithful.

The next kind of person is proclaimed as 'sorcerers.' We are surrounded today by the occult and witchcraft. Through films and evil books children as well as adults are being indoctrinated with witchcraft, which is just another word for sorcery. Spiritism is not spiritual. It is demonism. No one receives messages from the dead, but demons impersonate dead people. Many people around the world worship idols and images. This is strictly forbidden in God's Word, and the apostle Paul was confronted with demonism or sorcery in his day. In Acts 19 we learn that some of these people were converted, and in verse 19 we read 'Many of them also which used curious arts brought their books together, and burned them before all men.' A young Christian friend of mine who had paid a thousand pounds for a certain object as an investment recently destroyed it entirely, because it was Satanic. No child of God should keep Satanic objects in their home. In Deuteronomy 18:10-12 the Lord openly condemns witchcraft. Satan never gives joy, just eventual heartache and an eternity in hell. Listen to the words of Charles Weigle:-

> All my life was full of sin when Jesus found me,
> All my heart was full of misery and woe!
> Jesus placed His strong and loving arms around me,
> And He led me in the way I ought to go.

The blood of the Lord Jesus was shed for sinners who dabble in witchcraft and the occult. Remember the Word of God in Exodus 12:13: 'When I see the blood, I will pass over you.'

The next word is 'idolaters.' We have already spoken about idol worship. But what does God's commandment say? Exodus 20:3-4 states, 'Thou shalt have no other gods before Me. Thou shalt not make unto thee any graven image.' Idol worship is strictly forbidden, yet many poor Roman Catholic and pagan people bow down before statues and stupidly pray to them. Idol worshippers are going to the lake of fire. Do you wish to go there?

The last description of the enormous company is the word 'liars.' Does that include us all? White lies and little lies are still lies. Bending the truth is still lying. Satan is the father of lies. In John 8:44 the Lord Jesus told His hearers that Satan was a murderer and also the father of lies. Yet, we can praise the Lord that every confessed sin can be cleansed by the precious blood of the Saviour.

> Come ye sinners, lost and hopeless,
> Jesus blood can make you free;
> For He saved the worst among you
> When He saved a wretch like me.

A TREMENDOUS VERSE

So much for The Enormous Company. Without Christ they are all going to the Lake of Fire. Let us look now a little farther into this text. We see here:-

THE EMBITTERED CONSEQUENCE

'But the fearful, and unbelieving, and the abominable and murderers, and whoremongers, and sorcerers, and idolaters, and all liars, shall have their part in the lake which burneth with fire and brimstone.' Notice these words: 'shall have their part.' The Bible is saying very clearly that this is the embittered consequence of sinning and going one's own way. Dr Lehman Strauss points out that such sinners 'cannot enter the new order of the redeemed. They would sow seeds of sin, wickedness and corrupt the new heavens and the new earth. Therefore, their place is in the place of torment with the Antichrist and the False Prophet who will already be there. Satan will join them later. This is the eternal doom of all who do not receive the Lord Jesus Christ as their personal Saviour.'

The Bible says in Romans 5:8 'God commendeth His love toward us, in that, while we were yet sinners Christ died for us.' Yes, friend, 'God so loved the world that He gave His only begotten Son that whosoever believeth in Him should not perish, but have everlasting life.' Have you, friend, tasted of the wonderful love of the Lord? The Lord Jesus Christ put by all the glory that was His in heaven, and He came to this old world of ours deliberately to pay the price of our sin. He died in your place and mine. His blood was shed on the Cross at Calvary that you and I might be cleansed and forgiven.

Dr Lee Roberson in one of his books tells about a man who was soon to pass into eternity. The preacher asked him if he was ready, and he replied that he had been a good husband and a kind father. He had never intentionally wronged anyone. The preacher then said to him 'What kind of a place do you think heaven is?' The man thought and said it would be a place of much singing. There would be no sin and sorrow. He knew a little, but the evangelist then said to him that Revelation 1:5 indicates that the great song will be this:

'Unto Him who loved us, and washed us from our sins in His Own blood.' The man knew nothing of the saving and cleansing power of the blood of Jesus until that moment. Friend, where do you stand in this matter? Are you saved? Are you ready, or are you still one of the enormous company?

The embittered consequence of rejecting the way of salvation, and rejecting God's beloved Son will only lead to much bitterness for all eternity. Just now, you can be saved – but only if you repent and cry to the Lord for salvation. Listen to the words of the hymn:-

'Twas Jesus, my Saviour, Who died on the tree,

To open a fountain for sinners like me,

His blood is the fountain that pardon bestows,

And cleanses the foulest wherever it flows.

Repent now, dear friend, and be saved. 'Now is the accepted time; behold, now is the day of salvation' (2 Corinthians 6:2). Our text states 'But the fearful, and unbelieving, and the abominable, and murderers, and whoremongers, and sorcerers, and idolaters, and all liars, shall have their part in the lake which burneth with fire and brimstone, which is the second death.' Notice the last half of the text. It speaks of:-

THE EVERLASTING COST

Yes, friend, the everlasting cost of rejecting the Lord Jesus Christ, or simply being indifferent to Him, means eternity in hell – 'the lake which burneth with fire and brimstone.' How terrible! Is that where you wish to spend eternity? In Psalm 9:17 the Lord says, 'The wicked shall be turned into hell.' You may say that you are not wicked, but in the Lord's eyes we are all wicked until we are saved and cleansed by the precious blood of the Lord Jesus. Hell was not prepared for people in the first place, for it was intended for the devil and his followers. However, all who reject the Saviour will go there. Just think, God loved us so much that He did not wish anyone to go there, so He sent His only begotten Son into the world to pay the price of our sin.

A TREMENDOUS VERSE

The everlasting cost of being indifferent to the love of God as revealed in the Lord Jesus is spending endless millions of years in the place of torment. In Luke 16 the Lord Jesus Christ told the true story of a rich man who died and went to the place of endless torment. Verse 23 says, 'And in hell he lifted up his eyes, being in torments.' Hell has a way in, but no way out.

In Matthew 23 the Lord Jesus was addressing the religious leaders of His day, the scribes and the Pharisees, and He said to them 'How can ye escape the damnation of hell?' Friend, there *is* a way of escape: Jesus! Repent of all your sin now and ask Him to save you, and He will. The Lord Jesus described hell as a place of outer darkness – a place of weeping and wailing and endless torment. Is that what you look for, friend? Without the Lord Jesus as your own personal Saviour, that is your destiny.

The everlasting cost is endless punishment which will never end. The vast majority are going there. Jesus, when describing the way to heaven and the way to hell said 'Wide is the gate, and broad is the way, that leadeth to destruction, and many there be which go in thereat' (Matthew 7:13). Hell is a place of separation from all that is lovely. It will be a lonely place for all who have born again relations, for they will never see them again.

Hell or the Lake of Fire is everlasting. Do you honestly wish to go there? The Bible says 'Whosoever shall call on the name of the Lord shall be saved' (Romans 10:13). Will you make that call NOW while you have time? The everlasting cost of not bothering is HELL – the Lake of Fire and brimstone. Do you not wish to escape? Listen to the words of the hymn:-

    Time is now fleeting, the moments are passing –

    Passing from you and from me;

    Shadows are gathering, deathbeds are coming –

    Coming for you and for me!

Where, friend, are YOU going? That hymn goes on to say:-

    Oh for the wonderful love He has promised –

    Promised for you and for me!

Though we have sinned, He has mercy and pardon –
Pardon for you and for me!
Will you come and receive the Saviour now?

CHAPTER TWENTY-ONE

THE NEW JERUSALEM

Reading: Revelation 21:9-27 and 22:1-5

Text: Revelation 21:10: 'He carried me away in the spirit to a great and high mountain, and shewed me that great city, the holy Jerusalem, descending out of heaven.'

INTRODUCTION

Revelation chapters 21 and 22 deal with seven new things. In our reading we are confronted with the New Jerusalem. This great city is yet future. No doubt its preparation is nearly complete. How do we know this? In John's Gospel chapter 14, the Lord Jesus told His followers 'I go to prepare a place for you.' Today He is completing the preparations for the coming of His bride, the Church. It is the 'place of many mansions.' It is the place where all who are saved are going to live. It is a wonderful place, for the Word of God gives us some information about it.

It is important that we are sure we are going there. How can we be sure? Simply by making certain that we have repented of all our sin and asked the Lord Jesus Christ to save us. Without His salvation there is no hope. 'Christ Jesus came into the world to save sinners' (1 Timothy 1:15). Are you, friend, saved? Are you bound for heaven? Let us look now for a little at the New Jerusalem.

THE DESCENT OF THE CITY

The Bible tells us that John was taken by one of the seven special angels to a great and high mountain, in the spirit. This is what he saw: 'that great city, the holy Jerusalem, descending out of heaven from God.' It was coming down – descending from heaven. It was not being built or created on the earth, but it was all ready, and God the Father was sending it down. This is a place that has been prepared somewhere. We do not exactly know where, but the Bible says it is to come from God out of heaven. Man today does not know where heaven is precisely located, but if the New Jerusalem is to come down, then heaven must be up!

Heaven is certainly not on the earth. Therefore it must be up! The Bible does give clues as to this. When Satan rebelled he was cast down from heaven. Look at Isaiah 14:12-14. 'How art thou fallen from heaven, O Lucifer, son of the morning! How art thou cut down to the ground . . . For thou hast said in thine heart, I will ascend into heaven, I will exalt my throne above the stars of God: I will sit also upon the mount of the congregation, in the sides of the north: I will ascend above the heights of the clouds; I will be like the Most High.' So, we see that heaven is *up,* and Satan was cast *down.* Heaven also would seem to be somewhere in the North. Wherever it is, the Lord is today preparing this great city, the New Jerusalem. It is going to descend.

Let us consider, secondly,

THE DESCRIPTION OF THE CITY

From verse 11 onward, Revelation 21 describes the New Jerusalem. First of all, we are told it is full of the glory of God. It is very bright, for John tells us its light was 'like a stone most precious, even like a jasper stone, clear as crystal.' So, it won't be a dull place. It will be dazzlingly bright! This city will have twelve gates, three on each side of the city. Each gate will have an angel guarding it, and the gates will be named after the twelve tribes of Israel.

THE NEW JERUSALEM

The description of the city tells us that it is to be fifteen hundred miles long, fifteen hundred miles wide and fifteen hundred miles high. It would appear to be a cube, but Clarence Larkin, the great Bible teacher and scholar thinks it might be a pyramid. Anyway, the Bible does not clarify this point.

The wall is to be 216 feet high. This wall will be magnificent for it will be garnished with many precious stones. The twelve gates will be made of pearl. The streets will shine with pure gold. The foundations will shine, as there will be twelve different types of these, all made of precious stones.

During the Millennial reign of the Lord Jesus there will be a temple for the worship of God the Father. The Lord Jesus will be reigning, but His desire will be for people to worship His Father. Christians today worship the Father, through the Son and by the Holy Spirit. When the New Jerusalem is established, there will be no temple. Why is this? John tells us in verse 22: 'I saw no temple therein: for the Lord God Almighty and the Lamb are the temple of it.' You see, God the Father is going to make His residence with His people in the New Jerusalem. He and the Lord Jesus Christ will be the temple – the place of endless worship and praise.

As we look further at the description, we learn about the new light. Light today comes from the sun, and at night from the moon and stars. In the New Jerusalem things will be vastly different. Verse 23 tells us 'The city had no need of the sun, neither of the moon, to shine in it: for the glory of God did lighten it, and the Lamb is the light of it.' Have we not sung the hymn 'The Light of the World is Jesus'? I wonder, friend, do you all know Him in this way? So many people today walk in darkness. The Lord Jesus claimed that he was and is *the Light*. Those who do not know Him need to repent of all their sin and ask Him to come into their hearts and save them. Salvation is only through Christ. There is no other way to be saved eternally.

'The Lamb' refers to the Lord Jesus Christ. John the Baptist introduced Him in John 1:29 in this way. 'Behold the Lamb of God, which taketh away the sin of the world.' John knew why the Lord Jesus had come. He came to save sinners. Paul tells us the same in 1 Timothy 1:15: 'Christ Jesus came into the world to save sinners.' Are you, friend, saved? Get to know this precious Lamb of God – the One Who 'loved me, and gave Himself for me' (Galatians 2:20).

> Ye dwellers in darkness, with sin-blinded eyes,
> The Light of the world is Jesus!
> Go, wash at His bidding, and light will arise,
> The Light of the world is Jesus!
> No need of the sunlight in heaven, we're told,
> The Light of the world is Jesus!
> The Lamb is the Light in the city of gold,
> The Light of the world is Jesus!

The New Jerusalem will be a wonderful place. Psalm 16:11 states 'In Thy presence is fullness of joy.' We who shall live in the New Jerusalem will be living in the constant presence of the Lord, in a state of constant joy. Ephesians 1:10 tells us that it will be a place of complete unity. There will be no sin, no sadness, no sickness and no sorrow. The late Dr DeHaan wrote this: 'Can you imagine what this glorious sight will be? Picture a new earth on which dwells the restored and redeemed nation of Israel, and around them are literal nations of redeemed people, consisting of the saved of the nations which came through the Millennium. All dwell on the new earth. Hanging over that new earth, suspended in the sky, is this gigantic city, the New Jerusalem, the inhabitation of the Bride of Christ.'

This city will be fabulous! We have looked at The Descent of the City and the Description of the City. Let us now look at:-

THE DWELLERS IN THE CITY

We need to go back to verse 9. Here we find the angelic messenger telling John 'Come hither, I will shew thee the bride, the Lamb's wife.' As we have seen already, the Lamb is the Lord Jesus Christ. His wife is the true church – that body of men and women, boys and girls, who have been redeemed. The

Church commenced on the Day of Pentecost and all those saved by the grace of God since that day compose the Bride of Christ. The Old Testament believers are not included, for they are referred to in the Bible as 'friends of the Bridegroom.' They will have their place in God's plan, but the Church is that special body – 'the body of Christ', as Paul calls it. So, we see that all the saved ones will be the dwellers in the city, along with the Lord Jesus Christ and His Father, our eternal God. Revelation 22:3 states, 'The throne of God and of the Lamb shall be in it.' Dr Lehman Strauss, describing the New Jerusalem, says 'We shall behold Him in His glorified body in the Person of Jesus Christ. Peter, James and John caught a glimpse of His deity when He was transfigured before them on the holy mount, but we shall behold Him in the full display of His glory throughout eternity.'

The Dwellers in the City will all be born again. In John 3:3 the Lord Jesus told the chief religious leader of His day 'Except a man be born again, he cannot see the kingdom of God.' Unsaved ones will not make it to heaven, and no unsaved ones will ever live in the New Jerusalem. It is fully booked – booked for the Bride of Christ.

At times we who love the Lord are despised and ridiculed, and in some countries persecuted and put to death. In the New Jerusalem we shall reign with the Lord Jesus Christ, not just for a few brief years, but for ever and ever. Revelation 22:4 and 5 describes The Dwellers in the City: 'They shall see His face; and His name shall be in their foreheads. And there shall be no night there; and they need no candle, neither light of the sun, for the Lord God giveth them light: and they shall reign for ever and ever.' What a prospect!

All of us who are saved can rejoice today in our great salvation. The Lord has saved us from our sin. He has promised us an eternal home. As part of the Bride of Christ we shall live eventually in the New Jerusalem, and reign with Christ, and be with Him for ever and ever. Is everyone reading this saved? Is everyone reading this washed in the precious blood of the Lamb? His blood made a perfect atonement for our sin. The Lord Jesus went to Calvary with one purpose only: to atone for our sin. Just before He gave up His life He cried with a loud voice 'Tetelestai' – 'Finished.' HE had completed the work of redemption. He was not finished, but He had accomplished His atoning work.

Romans 5:19 points out 'By one man's disobedience many were made sinners, so by the obedience of One shall many be made righteous.' Through the Lord Jesus Christ, and through Him alone, we can be saved. No church or religion can help, only Christ.

The Dwellers in the City can well sing the words of the lovely hymn:-

Jesus is all the world to me,

My life, my joy, my all;

He is my strength from day to day;

Without Him I would fall.

When I am sad to Him I go,

No other one can cheer me so;

When I am sad He makes me glad –

He's my Friend.

If you do not know this Friend, come now and trust Him as your Saviour. We have one final thought. In the New Jerusalem, there will be:-

NO DEFILEMENT IN THE CITY

We have considered briefly The Descent of the City, The Description of the City and The Dwellers in the City. However, Revelation 21:27 indicates clearly that there will be No Defilement in the City. 'There shall in no wise enter into it anything that defileth, neither whatsoever worketh abomination, or maketh a lie: but they which are written in the Lamb's book of life.' No sinner will be allowed to enter that wonderful city. Only blood-washed people. Just saved sinners. The Bible says 'They which are written in the Lamb's book of life.' This phrase, the Lamb's book of life' is used a number of times in Revelation. Revelation 20:15 states 'Whosoever was not found written in the book of life was cast into the lake of fire.' That place is where the unsaved are

THE NEW JERUSALEM

eventually going – hell, the lake of fire – where they will be tormented for ever and ever. In Philippians 4:4 Paul reminds believers that their names are in 'the book of life.' It is quite clear from the Bible that whenever a person truly repents of all their sin and asks the Lord Jesus to save them and cleanse them with His precious blood, their names are written in His book of life. This book is His personal possession, for it records the names of all who will eventually form His Bride.

We have to note this seriously. *No unwashed sinner* will be allowed into the New Jerusalem. No one will be permitted to cause any form of sin in this city. No forms of evil, no witchcraft, no satanic things will ever be permitted to enter. The twelve guards – the angels at the gates – will see to it that all is lovely and perfect.

DL Moody told the story of a group of holiday makers who arrived at a hotel, hoping for accommodation. When they were told that it was full, they turned away to try elsewhere. One of the party remained. She had made her own reservation ahead of travel. Have you, my friend, made such a reservation? Or, will you be excluded from the New Jerusalem? You can make sure now of being there, by repenting now and asking the Lord to save you. It would be tragic to miss living for all eternity in that wonderful city. Make sure your name is in 'the book of life' today.

> Is your name written there in the Lamb's book of life?
> When you leave this old world with its sin and its strife,
> Will they find your name there –
> 'Mongst the ransomed of God –
> In the Lamb's Book of Life
> Through the Lamb's precious blood?
>
> (J Danson Smith)

CHAPTER TWENTY-TWO

THE BEGINNING AND THE END

Reading: Revelation 22:8-21

Text: Revelation 22:13: 'I am Alpha and Omega, the beginning and the end, the first and the last.'

INTRODUCTION

The last chapter of the Bible has a great message. In fact, it has several important messages which apply to people today.

John, the apostle, was greatly affected by all that he had seen, and the angel who was with him told him not to seal up what he had seen but to reveal it all to the world, as they needed to know. Today, as never before, we need to proclaim the fact that the Lord Jesus Christ is coming again. Can I ask, friend, are you ready? The Bible says 'The time is at hand.' Our text for this chapter is simply 'I am Alpha and Omega, the beginning and the end, the first and the last.' Let us look for a little at this wonderful passage of Scripture. Note first of all:-

THE INSPIRING PROCLAMATION

'I am Alpha and Omega.' These words may mean nothing to some people, but these words, Alpha and Omega, are the first and last letters of the Greek alphabet. Just as A and Z are our first and last letters, so in the Greek in which the New Testament was written, Alpha begins the alphabet, and Omega ends it. Here we have the inspiring proclamation that the Lord Jesus Christ is first and last.

When we look at Genesis 1:1, we read 'In the beginning God created the heaven and the earth.' The word for 'God' here is 'Elohim', which is plural and thus refers to the Trinity. When we turn to John 1:1 we find these words: 'In the beginning was the Word (the Lord Jesus) and the Word was with God, and the Word was God.' Verse 3 states 'All things were made by Him, and without Him was not any thing made that was made.' So, we find that the Lord Jesus Christ was the creator. He was indeed the first – the Alpha. Christian friend, is He first in your life?

The Trinity is a mystery which we have to accept, although no doubt it will be explained fully in our eternal state. Paul says in Colossians 2:9 'In Him dwelleth all fullness of the Godhead bodily.' Christ is First and Christ is also Last.

This inspiring proclamation reminds us that the last event on earth for the Christians who remain is the coming again of the Lord Jesus Christ. He most certainly is returning. He promised many times that He would come again. This chapter finishes with the Lord's clear promise 'Surely, I come quickly.' This word 'quickly' means suddenly – rapidly – in a flash – without warning. If we look at Matthew 24 we find the Lord Jesus telling people in verse 42, 'Watch therefore: for ye know not what hour your Lord doth come.' And a couple of verses further on He says 'Therefore be ye also ready: for in such an hour as ye think not the Son of man cometh.' The apostle Paul tells us in 1 Corinthians 15:51 and 52: 'Behold I shew you a mystery; we shall not all sleep, but we shall all be changed, in a moment, in the twinkling of an eye.' The Rapture of the Church – all who are born again – will be the last event for us here on earth, and that great event could happen today.

What an inspiring proclamation! As the hymnwriter put it:-

> He comes! He comes! Oh, blest anticipation,
> In keeping with His true and faithful word;

To call us to our heavenly consummation –
Caught up – to be for ever with the Lord.
Let us notice, secondly,

THE INTIMATED PROMISE

In verse 14 we read the intimated promise. 'Blessed are they that do His commandments, that they may have right to the tree of life, and may enter in through the gates into the city.' What a promise! And to whom does this promise apply? Who are they that do His commandments? The Bible makes it clear that only those whose names are written in heaven will ever enter the New Jerusalem. So, it is saved people who inherit the intimated promise. Are you saved? Have you been washed in the blood of the Lamb? If not, then now is the time to repent and ask the Lord to save you. The Bible says in various places 'Whosoever shall call on the name of the Lord shall be saved.' Our text states 'I am Alpha and Omega, the beginning and the end.' The Lord Jesus Christ came to save, and when we trust Him our life really begins. And, as we live for Him and seek to serve Him, He is also the end! We live for Him, not self.

The apostle Paul wrote 'To me to live is Christ' (Philippians 1:21). He should be our central thought in life, and His intimated promise guarantees us access to our dwelling place in the Holy City. Good works and righteous living will get no one a place in heaven. No, it is reserved for sinners saved by grace. Religion cannot save, for only Christ can. Salvation is offered freely to all, for it is God's gift – a gift we should never refuse. The Bible says in Romans 6:23, 'The gift of God is eternal life through Jesus Christ our Lord.' Have *you* received this gift? We offer it now to you. Believe and be saved.

The tree of life is mentioned in Genesis and although Adam and Eve were not to touch it, it will be there in heaven for all believers to enjoy. Eternal life is promised to every one who is saved. On the Cross at Calvary, the Lord Jesus Christ made full atonement for our sins. He suffered on that old tree – crucified, His head crowned with thorns, His side bleeding – and He went through all that for us poor, lost sinners. The hymnwriter reminds us in these words:-

> He has made a full atonement,
> Now His saving work is done;
> He has satisfied the Father,
> Who accepts us in His Son.
> But remember, this same Jesus
> In the clouds will come again;
> And with Him His blood-bought people
> Evermore with Him to reign.

'I am Alpha and Omega, the beginning and the end.' All who are saved by God's grace will not only have access to the New Jerusalem, but will live in it with their Saviour, the Lord Jesus Christ.

Notice, thirdly, there is:-

AN INCLUSIVE PRAYER

We see this in verse 17. It says, 'The Spirit and the bride say, Come. And let him that heareth say, Come. And let him that is athirst Come. And whosoever will, let him take the water of life freely.' Here is the prayer of the Holy Spirit and the desire of the church – all true believers – praying that people will come and be saved. The Lord Jesus is the Alpha and the Omega, and men and women, and boys and girls need to get to know Him and trust Him as their personal Saviour. People who are saved pray for the Lord to come soon, but we need also to pray for the unsaved to repent and come to the Lord. The great Bible teacher, Dr MR DeHaan says of this verse that all Christians who have read the Book of Revelation and understood the terrors which lie ahead should be crying out to a lost world 'COME.' When, Christian friend, did you last invite someone to come to a Gospel meeting, and when did you invite someone to come to Christ?

THE BEGINNING AND THE END

'I am Alpha and Omega, the beginning and the end.' When we give out this invitation 'Come', the Alpha is with us. He will never fail us. This is the absolute duty and responsibility of every Christian: to tell others to come and be saved. Do we wish our unsaved friends and loved ones to go to hell? It is their permanent destination if they are not saved. Do we pray for their salvation? Are we truly concerned? The Lord needs to burden us with this matter. If the Lord's dear people were truly concerned they would fill the churches which preach the Gospel with unsaved friends and relatives.

Dr. Lee Roberson, in one of his books, tells how two men travelled to work on the same train every day for many years. One went to church on Sunday mornings, but the other went nowhere. The day came when this man became very ill. His wife was a Christian and she was very anxious. She said to her husband, 'Will I get a Christian to come and speak to you?' The husband said 'No. I have travelled for many years on the train with John. He goes to church, but he never speaks about it, so I don't think there is anything in it.' The man died without a Saviour. The Inclusive Prayer of the Holy Spirit and the church is 'COME.' People need to come for a cleansing in Calvary's tide and be washed in the blood of the Lamb.

Unsaved friend, will you come now and be saved? Christian friend, will you start praying in earnest for people you know to get saved? The Lord Jesus Christ is the 'Alpha and Omega', so He expects every child of God to be faithful and work for Him. That is the way to revival.

> Revive Thy work, O Lord;
> While here to thee we bow;
> Descend, O gracious Lord, descend!
> Oh, come and bless us now!

We have seen The Inspiring Proclamation, The Intimated Promise and the Inclusive Prayer. Look next at:-

THE INERRANT PROPHECY

Verse 19 states 'If any man shall take away from the words of the book of this prophecy, God shall take away his part out of the book of life, and out of the holy city.' What a serious statement.

Anyone who denies the Word of God and ridicules in particular the Book of Revelation with all its forecasts, will be sent to hell for ever and ever. It is deadly to deny the Word of God.

The Bible is inerrant. It is absolutely true from cover to cover. All of it is fully inspired. It claims this for itself in 2 Peter 1:21 where it says 'Holy men of God spake (wrote) as they were moved by the Holy Ghost.' Then, in 1 Peter 1:25 Peter wrote, 'The word of the Lord endureth for ever. And this is the word which by the gospel is preached unto you.'

What is the Gospel? It is good news – the great news that the Alpha and Omega, the Lord Jesus Christ, came to save sinners. He entered this world in order to pay the price of sin. The first act of sin was in the Garden of Eden, related to us in Genesis. However, in Genesis 3:15, the Lord promised Eve that her Seed (the Lord Jesus Christ) would defeat Satan eventually. This was the first promise of salvation in the Word of God. The coming of Christ was first promised here in Genesis 3. All through the Bible the work of redemption is made clear. Christ and Christ alone could save. Romans 5:12 says 'By one man (Adam) sin entered into the world, and death by sin.' Further on in this chapter, Paul says in verse 19 'For as by one man's disobedience many were made sinners, so by the obedience of One (the Lord Jesus Christ) shall many be made righteous.'

The atoning death of the Saviour made full atonement for sin. No one else could do this. No money, no other religion, no other person could make atonement, but the Lord Jesus did. How wonderful! But, people who deny this or disbelieve it are doomed for a lost eternity. The Bible is God's infallible, inerrant Word, and all who disbelieve it are doomed. Unsaved friend, where do you stand? Do you laugh at the Bible? Do you mock at the thought of hell?

THE BEGINNING AND THE END

Remember the words: 'God shall take away his part.' Oh, my friend, repent and come to the Saviour now. He is 'the Alpha and Omega.'

We have one final thought. It is this:-

THE INDESCRIBABLE PLEASURE

Verse 20 gives us these words 'He which testifieth these things saith, Surely I come quickly.' This is the thrilling finish to God's wonderful Word. Jesus is coming again. And, He is coming suddenly. Are you ready? We live in a world of darkness and sin. Things get rapidly worse and worse, but for the Christian we have a hope – rather, we have this indescribable pleasure for which we wait. As Paul wrote to the young church at Thessalonica 'We look for God's Son from heaven, Whom He raised from the dead, even Jesus, Which saved us from the wrath to come' (1 Thessalonians 1:10). Paul, and these Christians knew that when they trusted the Saviour there would never be a chance of them going to hell. It is wonderful to be saved, and our joy will be indescribable when we see for the first time the One Who went to Calvary to die in our place and take our punishment for us!

The Bible ends with His Own personal promise that He is coming again. One of these days the trumpet will sound and the Christian dead will be raised and all the living Christians will be caught up to meet the Lord in the air. This is our hope. The Lord Jesus Christ is coming soon! This will be the Omega part – the end for us on earth, and our new life with Christ in the eternal state will begin. New bodies which will never know pain or suffering will be ours, and we shall live for ever with Him. 'I am the Alpha and Omega, the beginning and the end, the first and the last.'

We cannot commence to imagine the indescribable pleasure which will be the lot of the Christian when they see Jesus. This wonderful book – Revelation – commences with the promise 'Behold, He cometh with clouds, and every eye shall see Him' (Revelation 1:7). That is the day when the Lord Jesus comes back to reign. In this last chapter there is the great invitation to all who are not yet Christians: 'Come.' Will YOU come now and repent of all your sin and ask the Lord to save you? This is your chance, perhaps the last one, to get saved. This is the end of the Bible and this is the final warning. Repent now and be saved. The Bible says 'The blood of Jesus Christ, His Son, cleanseth us from all sin' (1 John 1:7). The Lord Jesus is the Alpha and Omega – the beginning and the end of our salvation.

> Come, oh come, while Christ is calling,
> Linger not in paths of sin;
> Sever every tie that binds you;
> And the heavenly race begin.

Unsaved friend, come NOW. Remember, He is the Alpha and Omega – the ONLY Saviour.

PERHAPS TODAY!

> Look up and long for our dear Lord's returning!
> Look up and cry 'Lord Jesus come' we pray!
> Look up – until for Him the heart is burning!
> Look up! Look up! Perhaps He'll come today!
>
> (J Danson Smith)

'The Coming of the Lord draweth nigh' (James 5:8).

ABOUT THE AUTHOR

Theodore C. Danson Smith was born into a Christian home in Edinburgh, Scotland. At the early age of five he trusted the Lord Jesus Christ as his own personal Saviour. On his sixth birthday he received a card from a friend in the U.S.A. with the words written on it 'There was a man sent from God whose name was Theodore.' This came as a clear call from God that he was to preach the Gospel, and these words 'sent from God' guided his whole life.

Theodore has spent his whole life in Christian literature work at B. McCall Barbour, Edinburgh, as well as engaging in much evangelism. He spent over sixteen years of study in his spare time to gain qualifications in the Bible and Theology. As a preacher he is well known throughout Great Britain.

Theodore has no time for the Ecumenical Movement, modern versions of the Bible or the Charismatic movement. His Message is very clear: 'Believe on the Lord Jesus Christ and thou shalt be saved' (Acts 16:31).

Theodore's earlier books have proved to be a blessing to the Lord's people. A number of readers have reported that they came to saving faith in Christ through reading his books.

For more information about

Theodore C. Danson Smith
and
Snapshots from the Book of Revelation
please contact:
B. McCall Barbour
28 George IV Bridge
Edinburgh
EH1 1 ES
Scotland

For more information about
AMBASSADOR INTERNATIONAL
please visit:

www.ambassador-international.com
@AmbassadorIntl
www.facebook.com/AmbassadorIntl

If you enjoyed this book, please consider leaving us a review on Amazon, Goodreads, or our website.